THE LITERATURE OF PHOTOGRAPHY

THE LITERATURE OF PHOTOGRAPHY

Advisory Editors:

PETER C. BUNNELL
PRINCETON UNIVERSITY

ROBERT A. SOBIESZEK
INTERNATIONAL MUSEUM OF PHOTOGRAPHY
AT GEORGE EASTMAN HOUSE

THE STUDIO:

AND

WHAT TO DO IN IT

BY

H. P. ROBINSON

ARNO PRESS
A NEW YORK TIMES COMPANY

NEW YORK ★ 1973

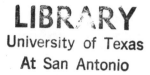
Reprint Edition 1973 by Arno Press Inc.

Reprinted from a copy in
  The George Eastman House Library

The Literature of Photography
ISBN for complete set: 0-405-04889-0
See last pages of this volume for titles.

Manufactured in the United States of America

———◆———

Library of Congress Cataloging in Publication Data

Robinson, Henry Peach, 1830-1901.
  The studio: and what to do in it.

  (The Literature of photography)
  Reprint of the 1891 ed.
  1. Photography--Studios and darkrooms. 2. Photo-
graphy--Portraits. I. Title. II. Series.
TR550.R6 1973   770'.28   72-9231
ISBN 0-405-04937-4

THE STUDIO,

AND WHAT TO DO IN IT.

THE STUDIO:

AND

WHAT TO DO IN IT.

BY

H. P. ROBINSON,

AUTHOR OF

"Pictorial Effect in Photography," "Picture Making by Photography," &c., &c.

LONDON:

PIPER & CARTER, 5, FURNIVAL STREET, HOLBORN, E.C.

1891.

LONDON:
PIPER AND CARTER, PRINTERS, FURNIVAL STREET, HOLBORN, E.C.

PREFACE.

My little books on the Art side of photography have been received with so much favour, that I venture to add another to the number. "PICTORIAL EFFECT" treated of art principles; "PICTURE MAKING" of the application of those principles to out-door photography; the present work is chiefly concerned with portraiture.

For in-door work a studio is essential. There have been so many different forms of studios invented, designed, or modified from others, that when a photographer wishes to build a studio, and turns to the authorities for information and guidance, he finds something very like chaos, for in the multitude of councillors there is—confusion. In the following chapters I have briefly described the leading types of studios, and devoted a chapter to a description of what a very long and varied experience, and the building of half-a-dozen studios for myself, and the designing of a large number for my friends, confirm me in thinking the best.

Throughout the book I have not attempted to recommend anything that is desirable but impossible, or to decry anything that I feel is not quite correct, but yet is part of the photographer's business to employ. For instance, I quite agree with the late Mr. Norman Macbeth, whose advice on art was always sound, that as the portrait is derived directly from living subjects, so should the backgrounds and surroundings be composed of real objects; but I know that in the practical business of a portrait photographer, it would be next to impossible to compass this desirable result, and therefore I have admitted the use of painted screens. The chapters on Posing and the Management of the Sitter embody the result of twenty-five years of daily work in the studio, and I trust will be of use to the professional photographer; and the concluding chapters will, I hope, aid him in other departments of his profession.

Although the great bulk of the book is new, I must acknowledge that some of the chapters have already appeared in the pages of the *Photographic News*, a journal which, without neglecting the strictly scientific detail upon which mechanical photography depends, has always urged upon photographers the study of art as of even more vital importance to success in their profession than science, which, after all, is only a similar means to a picture-making end as colour-making is to painters.

CONTENTS.

THE STUDIO,

AND WHAT TO DO IN IT.

CHAPTER I.

VARIOUS FORMS OF STUDIOS.

THE possession of a good studio goes quite half way to the production of good work, and its design and construction have been
a matter of anxious thought and earnest enquiry from the
earliest times of the art. A clever operator will, of course, get
presentable pictures even under difficulties, and it follows that
bad workmen will do bad work, however good their tools may be ;
but I hold that those who exercise any art should never have
their attention distracted from their work by defect of their
appliances, and the studio to a portrait photographer is an
appliance of the utmost importance. I propose, therefore, to
give a rapid sketch of the most important of the many forms of
studios that have been erected or proposed. Some of them may
have individual advantages not possessed by others, while in
many cases the form of studio adopted must be determined by
the space available; but from all of them it is possible that a
photographer about to build or alter a studio may get hints that
may be of use to him. I shall then give plans and descriptions
of a studio that I know from experience offers the greatest
advantages for every-day work.

It is a peculiarity of photographers to invent modifications;

this has not been confined to the chemical processes only, but
has extended to the studios in which those processes are
employed. The forms of studios—or glass-rooms, as they were
originally called—have exercised the ingenuity of their devisers
from the time of the discovery of photography. At first, as the
name implies, as much glass as possible was employed, and when
a clear space could be got for the erection, the studio was all
glass. As time went on, experience taught that a portrait could
be taken as quickly and with better results when less illumination was employed, and the area of the space admitting light
has been gradually reduced until a very little light, properly
directed, is now found sufficient for most purposes. The forms
taken by studios have been very numerous, and in some cases
quite fantastic, and have ranged in cost and style from that of
Aladdin's Palace to the meanest shanty. They have taken
that of the "lean-to," the ridge roof, the tunnel with many
variations, and amongst the eccentric kinds have been a
revolving studio, another looking like a gigantic accordion ;
and at one time, a domed or circular roof was strongly advocated,
under the erroneous impression that the curves of the dome would
concentrate the light, and make it more powerful. In addition
to this, it was once thought that, as effective light was composed
of the blue rays of the spectrum, blue glass would give more
light, and photographers glazed their studios with blue glass.
The ghastly effect on the sitter may be guessed, but the
advantages were not easily to be seen.

THE LEAN-TO.—Of all these designs, the lean-to and the
ridge-roof, or some modifications of them to suit the position
in which they are to be erected, are the only ones which have
retained the favour of photographers.

The lean-to is the most simple, and, where it can be built
against a high wall to protect it from the sun, one of the most
effective. It is particularly suited to small studios, those that
are not more than 11 or 12 feet wide. It is not necessary to

have the roof entirely of glass.   The following section gives the lines of a very useful small studio, that could be put up at very little expense.   If made about 25 feet long, it would be found all that an amateur could desire.   As a matter of lighting, I should prefer to omit the side light, and have the side solid, and two feet lower ; the light would then come from a low roof; but there are other things to think of.   In so narrow a studio, there would not be room for a full-sized background, which should

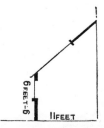

never be less than 8 feet high; and if the door is in the side, 6 feet 6 inches does not afford any too much height.

The RIDGE-ROOF is practically the same as the lean-to, differing only in the construction of the roof.   As the studio I shall describe in detail further on is a modification of the ridge-roof, I need not further describe it here.

Some of the earliest studios in London and other large towns were made by removing part of the roof of the garret of a house, and replacing it with glass ; and much excellent work has been done in these glass-rooms under most trying circumstances.   Of studios built under these conditions, that of the late T. R. Williams, of Regent Street, is a typical example.   Many photographers will remember that, in many qualities, and especially in delicacy and roundness of the perfect modelling, Williams's work was at the time unequalled.   For years his portraits were the wonder, envy, and admiration of all photographers.   Without recommending it for imitation, except where the exigencies of the situation make it necessary, I think an illustration and

description of this studio, written when Williams was at the
height of his fame, may be of interest to my readers, especially
as it shows to what an extent blinds have to be used when good
work has to be done under such worrying circumstances as
trouble the photographer when his studio is full in the sun.
The size of the room is about 30 feet long by 17 feet wide. As
will be seen from the woodcut, the chief light is from a skylight,
sloping in direction of the length of the room, not, as in the
ordinary lean-to roof, in direction of the width. The height at
the ridge is about 16 feet, at the eaves 8 feet. The glass covers

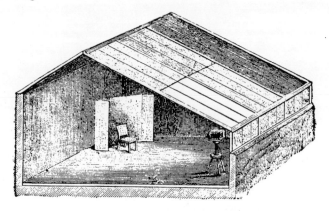

the whole of the longer side of the roof. The panes at the end
of the room are generally covered with blinds, so that the room
is lighted entirely from a skylight facing the south-west.

The sitter and the camera are placed cross-corner-wise of the
room, two backgrounds, one facing each corner towards the
light, being generally placed as fixtures. Some of these details
are omitted in the sketch, to give a clearer view of the interior.
Movable wings, covered with blue calico, are placed at each side
of the background, and at times are made to cut off direct light,
and at others to act as reflecting screens. The skylight is
furnished with three sets of blinds, each set consisting of three

blinds, one above another—one of dark blue calico, one of thick white calico, and another of thin white calico, or jaconet muslin. By the judicious management of these blinds almost any effect of lighting can be obtained. The diagram illustrates a mode of arrangement often used. Over one-third of the skylight, and half of the next third, the dark blue blinds are drawn, to exclude almost all light ; over the other half of the middle section a white blind is drawn, and also over the upper half of the remaining third. One-sixth of the skylight, and that the position most remote from the sitter, admits the light through clear glass ; and this, if the sun were shining, would be covered with the thin muslin blind. It will be seen that the principal light is often virtually a concentrated high side-light, the concentration giving effective cast shadows, whilst the amount of softened light admitted through thin blinds lights up the shadows, preventing blackness and hardness. Besides the blinds already described, there are two other dark blinds, which can, on occasion, be used. They are tolerably near to the head of the sitter, and can be used to prevent any vertical light reaching it. All the blinds are on spring rollers, placed near the top of the skylight, and can be readily drawn so as to cover any required portion of the roof.

The position and form of this studio could scarcely have been more awkward, or presented more difficulties to the operator, while the complication of three sets of blinds, besides screens, was enough to confuse any photographer ; but it was in the hands of an exceedingly able man, who produced some of the most delicate work that the world, up to that time, had seen ; hence other photographers, mistaking, as they often do, the materials for the man, thought that success lay in his collodion and baths and developers, and especially in his glass-room. This led to imitations which eventually grew into the many forms of tunnel studios, which were at one time excessively advocated, but soon abandoned.

An improvement on the form of the studio just described is

shown in that erected by an American photographer, which admits of side as well as top light. After the description given

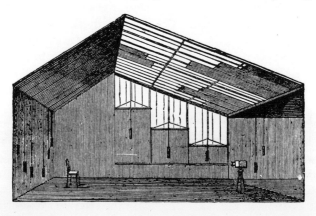

of Williams's studio, the illustration will speak sufficiently for itself.

The TUNNEL STUDIO is an illustration of the mischief clever photographers sometimes do by producing beautiful work under difficult circumstances. Williams, by the exercise of his great natural aptitude, patience, and skill, produces pictures with great technical beauties of light and shade. Rejlander, with a modification of the same kind of lighting, but with the addition of a tunnel in which to place his camera, realises many poetical ideas in photography; other photographers at once jump to the conclusion that it is all in the form of the studio, and build tunnels. Photographers, as I have already said, have an itching for modifications, and a mania for modifications of the tunnel set in. Every conceivable variation was resorted to to waste the money and spoil the tempers of photographers. The end of it all was, that every photographer who could afford it took down his costly experiments, and returned to the old-fashioned oblong room under a lean-to or ridge-roof. But it is well that anyone intending to construct a studio should at least hear of these experiments, especially as one of the objections to their use—length of exposure—no longer exists.

The earliest studios of this description seem to have been in form something like the Williams studio, but very much smaller, and with a dark place for the camera attached, from which they got their name. Here is a diagram and description of a small one erected by an amateur. The total length is 28 feet; of this, 4 feet at each side, and at the top at the background end as far as the ridge *b* B, is opaque, 10 feet glass, and the remaining portion, or tunnel, 14 feet wood. The height of the studio portion is 11 feet at *b*, and 7 feet at *c*, and 10 feet wide. The portion for the camera, in which there is no light, is 8 feet wide.

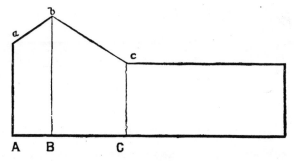

The side lights on each side have glass to the extent of 10 feet by 7 feet. The roof from *b* to *c* is glass. The opaque parts of the roof are of zinc. There is a door at each side at C, each of which, being opposite the other, admits of ready ventilation. A small dark room is erected in the unilluminated portion. The aspect of the studio is such that the sitter faces north-east, the studio having on the north and east an uninterrupted light, whilst the south and west lights are considerably excluded. The blinds are so arranged that light can be admitted from the right or left of the skylight as required.

The most important of the tunnel studios, and the one which attracted a great deal of attention at the time, was one erected by

Rejlander; it will be seen that very little light was admitted, a fault which would not be much felt now our processes are improved, but which was not found to be sufficient in the days of collodion for ordinary portraiture, and the light came from one side only, a fatal objection. Rejlander was famous for artistic studies, and one of the most striking things in his works was the great command he appeared to have over the lighting of the model. Almost every variety of lighting was adopted in turn to serve specific purposes, and always successfully. To the education of an artist Rejlander added years of practice as a photographer, not simply in manufacturing conventional portraits, but in producing art studies and complete pictures. His

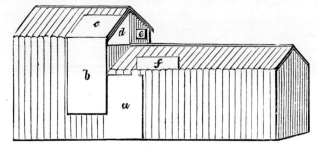

"Two Ways of Life" will be remembered as long as the art exists. In his practice he required a great variety of effects in lighting, but with all his marvellous skill and resource he found it difficult to get what he wanted in this form of studio, and was glad when circumstances compelled him to abandon it.

In designing this studio, the builder's chief aim was to secure a mode of lighting similar to that used by painters, so that the studio obtained may be available for painters; the same conditions of light and shadow existing in a photograph which are required in painting. That the same light would be often valuable for portraiture and general photography, there was no reason to doubt; the only misgiving being in the amount of light, which was found to be insufficient for any but the steadiest of sitters.

It had also the inconvenience, common to these studios, of being so strange and gloomy in effect as to materially interfere with the expression of the sitter.

It was built of corrugated iron; the total length was 30 feet. The portion devoted to the sitter was 10 feet long and 11 feet wide; the remaining 20 feet curving in near the door, and becoming narrower, so that, at the extreme end, where the dark room was, the width was 7 feet only. The light was obtained solely from the white spaces, *a, b, c, d, e, f*, in the diagram, the light falling from the north-west. The door, *a*, consisted of a plate of glass 7 feet high by 3 feet wide. The window adjoining, *b*, consisted of another plate of glass, 7 feet by 5 feet; this joined another plate, *c*, in the roof, which was 5 feet wide and 3 deep. These three were of white plate-glass, and constituted the chief source of light. On the opposite side there was no glass at all, but the interior was painted white to secure reflected lights. The minor lights, *d, e, f*, were generally covered with blinds, their object being to secure, not direct, but diffused light, to soften the shadows.

It will be seen that the sitter was lighted from the side and side-top, front light and direct vertical light being avoided. The camera was in comparative darkness, enabling the operator to focus without the aid of a cloth. The eye of the sitter also looked into darkness, a great advantage when we consider the dazzling effect of some of the studios of the time, but not of so much consequence now, when less light is used in all studios.

One of the most useful variations of the tunnel studio was that of Colonel Stuart Wortley. In this studio a much larger amount of light was admitted than with Rejlander's. On reference to the subjoined ground plan, it may be seen that the total length of the room was 36 feet; the portion really constituting the studio was 12 feet wide by 13 feet long. The unlighted portion, in which the camera stood, was 23 feet long by 8 feet wide.

The extreme end was divided off to form the dark room. The part marked 6 had a tier of shelves for various purposes.

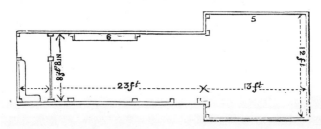

On reference to the sketch of the elevation, it will be seen that the studio portion was 12 feet high at the ridge. One side

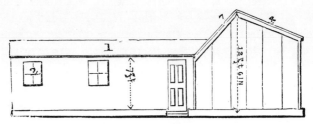

of the studio was all glass, consisting of corrugated glass from the ground to 7 feet high, and from thence to the roof clear glass.

This was a distinctive and valuable feature. The sloping front light (7) was clear glass. The opposite side of the studio was opaque, a reflected light only being obtained on that side. The roof (4) was also opaque. The only portions having glass were one side of the square or studio portion, and the front sloping portion of the roof (7). With the exception of the glazed portions, the room was chiefly constructed of inch boarding, roofed with asphalte felt. The un-illuminated portion was 7 feet high. The window, marked 2, was of orange glass for the dark room. Each pane of glass had a set of two blinds, one white, the other black, worked independent of each other.

There were many objections to the tunnel form of studio, the chief of which were as follows :—

When the blinds were drawn up, the light was a full front light, the worst that could be employed for portraiture. To get a well-lighted head, considerable knowledge of the effect of, and much trouble in the use of, blinds was necessary, and when the head was well lighted in one way—that is, when the modelling was good—it was badly lighted in another ; there was not enough light.

The variation in possible effects was limited. There was little opportunity of getting any other than the ordinary form of lighting. So-called Rembrandt effects were not common when the tunnel was in vogue, but they would have been very difficult to produce.

It was only suitable for taking single portraits. It was not adapted to groups of more than two or three persons, because if a group of figures occupied much space, one side would be well in the light, the other too much in shadow.

The general effect was gloomy in the extreme. The tunnel had a dreary, dungeon-like aspect, depressing to the sitter as well as to the operator.

As this is not a history of studio building, it is scarcely worth while to go into the details of other forms which have been taken by the glass-room. The question for practical photographers is, What is the best form of studio to build ? I hope to do something towards answering this important question in the next chapter.

CHAPTER II.

THE BEST FORM OF STUDIO.

It may sound not a little dogmatic to assert that anything is finally the best in this ever-changing and inventive world, where the finality of to-day is but the precursor of to-morrow's progress; but after many years' experience, and after a great deal of ingenuity and money have been spent in the endeavour to invent something new, practical photographers are still of opinion that for portrait studios no form has yet been invented to compare with that of which the lean-to and ridge-roof are types. It is on this general form that the studio I am about to describe and recommend is based.

That the best beginning to get at what we want is to discover what we require, is a truism none can dispute. Let us, then, try to arrive at what are the necessary points to consider in designing a well-appointed studio.

Experience has proved that the principle of excluding direct sunlight, and of working with diffused light, is the best. The interior of the building, therefore, should be well protected from the direct rays of the sun.

The arrangements for managing the light should be simple, so that they may be under the immediate and instant control of the operator; all complicated systems of blinds should be avoided.

Both ends of the studio should be available for use, so that the light may be directed on the sitter from the right or from the left.

The size of the studio should be large enough to admit of every necessary operation without inconvenience, but should not be so large as to become unmanageable or difficult to manage.

It should have a cheerful and homelike appearance, free from that look of an over-crowded work-room to which the studio is so often reduced.

It should be cool in summer, and comfortably warm in the winter.

Lastly.—The developing room and dressing rooms should be within convenient reach, the former commodious with sinks, tables, shelves, &c. The ventilation and light should be perfect.

THE DIMENSIONS.—The first thing to decide in designing a studio is the size. This will often be ruled by the space available; but we will assume that we have plenty of room. A large studio, like a great book, is a great evil. It is well to have plenty of space to move about in, and to contain the necessary furniture and accessories; but when a studio is above a certain size, it is found to be unwieldy and difficult to manage, and the lighting not so good as that found in smaller studios. The length may be partly determined by the size of picture to be taken, and it will be found that if the room is to be long enough to allow of a cabinet portrait to be taken of a full-length standing figure, with sufficient space for backgrounds, and a bit over for contingencies, 28 feet will be quite sufficient. In width, enough space should be left for a row of furniture along one side, and on the wall side for shelves, backgrounds, head-rest, &c. These necessary impedimenta on both sides will be found to take up 4 feet 6 inches, and if the width is made 14 feet, there will be left 9 feet 6 inches clear space for working. This could, of course, be increased, by removing furniture, to the full width of the room when necessary for taking large groups. This size is sufficient for all practical purposes. The photographer who goes in for very varied effects would find more space for background and accessories convenient; but it would be better to get this by an added room, rather than to interfere with the working part of the studio.

THE ANGLE OF THE SKYLIGHT.—A great deal of nonsense has been written upon the effect of the angle of glass through which the light is admitted. Some have held that if the pitch of the roof is high, the light will be refracted above the sitter's head; and if the roof be flat, the light will be directed to his feet. This has been learnedly demonstrated by the aid of diagrams, but is, nevertheless, not true. The amount of light will practically be found to depend on the size of the opening through which it is admitted, and, to some extent, to the nearness of the object to be photographed to that aperture, and the amount of sky to be seen from the sitter's chair.

The pitch of the glass roof of the ordinary ridge-roof studio usually takes an angle of 35° to 45°. When the roof is so flat as this angle indicates, and if the studio is not protected by a high building on its south side, the sun will be found to shine in, and be very annoying during most part of the day, and necessitate the employment of special blinds and other troublesome contrivances. A very little alteration of the pitch of the glass roof would remedy all this. As is well known by every schoolboy, the sun in our latitudes never attains a greater meridian altitude than 62° 30', as will be seen in the diagram at the end of this chapter (page 21), which shows the highest and lowest altitudes of summer and winter. If, then, the slope of the roof is made at the angle of the highest altitude (62° 30'), or still more upright, there would be no more trouble from the sun.

The kind of glass for glazing the skylight has been the subject of much controversy. Ordinary sheet glass is the best. It has the merit of being cheap, and has the further advantage of not being so liable to change to a yellow colour in the light as some other makes of glass. The size of the panes should be as large as the construction will admit. In the chapter on Lighting the Sitter, I mention ground glass for part of the roof; this should be referred to in connection with this subject.

The other dimensions to consider will be the height of the sides and the ridge. It has been usual to make the side-light 8 or 9 feet high to the eaves. This construction rendered it necessary to have much timber at the junction of the side and roof, a place where important light should be admitted without obstruction, and great stress used to be laid on the necessity of having low side-lights, so that the feet in a carte-de-visite may be properly lighted! We are wiser now. There is no use for the admission of any light lower than 4 feet 6 inches or 5 feet. We thus ascertain the height of the front wall to support the skylight; and if we determine that the height of the room to the ridge shall be 12 feet, we get the principal dimension, and the section of the room takes the form shown in the sketch (see page 21).

If the studio is placed against a building, it would be better to make the unglazed part a lead flat, which may be made useful for some purposes, such as printing, or it may be built on; but if the studio is in the open, then the roof may take the direction of the dotted line in the section, but the wall on which it rests must not be less than 8 feet high, or there will not be sufficient space to move backgrounds. The unequal sides give an ugly effect to the gable, but this, in most cases, can be broken by other buildings.

The light should have a northern aspect. If it incline to the north-east, so much the better. In the long days, however upright the skylight is constructed, the sun will shine into the studio in the early morning and in the evening. If the room is turned towards the north-east the sun will be off it before the studio is required for use, and will be better protected from its rays in the afternoon.

Both ends of the room should be backgrounds.

THE BLINDS should run easily, and the means of altering them be readily accessible. Spring rollers are good, but they sometimes get out of order. I have found it a good plan to make the blinds draw up with a clockweight. Blinds are more particularly referred to in the chapter on Lighting the Sitter.

THE APPEARANCE OF THE ROOM.—A great deal of the success of the portrait will depend on the effect of the photographer and his studio on the sitter. "Treatment" by the photographer is considered further on; it will be only necessary here to say a word or two on the appearance of the studio.

I prefer that the studio should have the effect of a moderately furnished living room, such as sitters may be expected to occupy in their own homes; avoiding shabbiness on the one hand, and ostentatious show on the other. Don't let there be a great display of anything, not even of your own good taste. The effect should come on the visitor as a matter of course. You will not be able to hide the implements of your art, nor is it desirable that you should do so. What I very much object to is that appearance of wreckage and lumber so often seen in studios. Your cameras, backgrounds, accessories must be there, but keep them in order. I like to keep the centre of my studio absolutely free, except for the camera, and perhaps a table or chair at the background end, and the furniture arranged along the walls ready for use when called upon. A cheerful effect has a great influence on many people. The tunnel was recommended for the singular reason that it would aid the expression; but it did just the reverse. There are people whose temperament will not allow them to look happy, however much they try, if they have to stare into a gloomy space. It is bad enough to be taken to a strange place and be made to go through a strange operation, without the additional discomfort of being taken into an uncomfortable room.

As a general principle, violent contrasts should be avoided in the furnishing of the studio, everything being kept as quiet and harmonious as possible. The wall paper should be simple and quiet in pattern, and of a warm grey in tone. The carpet is a difficulty. For appearance I should prefer to have it all over the room; but it offers resistance to the easy moving of backgrounds and furniture. It is better, therefore, to compromise the matter, and cover the floor with linoleum of a small, simple pattern, and have squares of carpet at both ends where the sitters are usually placed. It is easy now to obtain carpets of suitable pattern. Indian and Persian rugs are very useful. There should be a fixed background at each end; others may be stretched on frames set up on castors, so that they may be rapidly changed without effort.

THE TEMPERATURE AND VENTILATION should be carefully attended to. Many people are deterred from having their portraits taken for fear of the ordeal by heat in a photographer's stifling studio. It is pleasant to hear visitors say, as I often do, when they enter your studio in one of the broiling days of summer, "Why, this is the coolest place in the town!" Perfect comfort in the dog days can only be had when the studio has a high building on the south side. I once had a studio of the old ridge-roof form in which I suffered much from the heat, although the half towards the south was built solid. The southern side of the roof was slated, and became very hot. I cured this by putting up a wooden blind entirely

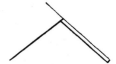

covering the slates, but fixed about a foot from them, so that a current of air should flow under the covering. The blind was carried higher than the roof, as shown in the sectional diagram.

It was found that the lighting was quite as quick and good as before, and this suggested placing the roof of any future studio at so upright an angle that the sun could not look over the ridge, even on the longest day.

THE DRESSING ROOM should be conveniently near the studio. I have known this room to be on one floor and the studio on another. This is very awkward, and likely to create confusion. A second room would be found useful.

AN ANTE-ROOM between the reception room and the studio would be found invaluable; it is useful to both ends. It is often advantageous to show some special picture away from the crowd of the general exhibition room, and it is especially useful to ask the friends of the sitter to go into while the sitting is taking place.

THE DEVELOPING ROOM.—No room is more neglected than this one. Any closet is thought good enough for a dark room; but no part of the establishment should call for more thought and attention. Health, comfort, eyesight, and, to a great extent, the quality of the work done, depend on this room. There should be sufficient space to conduct all the operations in comfort. Table space should be ample, and there should be sufficient shelves to hold everything but dust. The sinks used to be made of wood, lined either with gutta-percha or pitch, and were always causing trouble; white porcelain sinks were expensive, and could never be got large enough for all purposes. For several years I have used Doulton's sinks; they are made of glazed stoneware, are very cheap, can be got of any size, and are also useful for other purposes. I use one of them as a hypo dish, and a series of them for washing prints.

Perfect ventilation should be provided for. The dark room is not so stifling and unhealthy now as it was when collodion was used, but deleterious vapours still arise from the ammonia and other chemicals. This chapter is concerned more with design than construction, but the following sketch for a ventilator

may as well be given here.   It admits the air, but excludes
the light.   The arrangement consists of a long box of any length
required, with an opening (AB) all along the lower side of the
front, and a similar one (OP) all along the upper side at the back.
On the inside of the box two partitions (DD) are made; one extending from the bottom to within about 6 inches from the top,
and the other extending from the top to within about 6 inches
from the bottom.   The height of the box is about 1 foot 6
inches, and the depth from back to front is but little more.

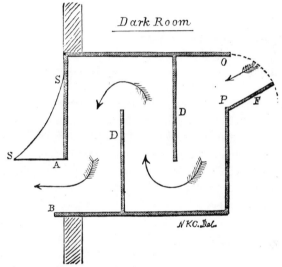

The opening in front (AB) should be the same with the space
left above and below the two partitions (DD), and also the same
as the opening (OP); the spaces, likewise, between the partitions and the back and front of the box, and between the two
partitions themselves, should be of the same size, viz., 6 inches.
A door at F is provided, to shut up to such a degree as may be
necessary.   The passage of the air through this apparatus is
shown by the arrows in the cut.   It will be obvious, from a
little consideration, that no light can enter the room through

the air-passage. SS is intended for an iron or zinc shade, fitted outside, if the apparatus be much exposed to the weather. It would also help to screen the light from the outside opening (AB). This ventilator, with a grating in the floor, ought to keep the air of the room pure.

THE LIGHT.—There is so much difference of opinion as to what light should be used to work by, that I feel considerable diffidence in giving any advice on the subject. In my own practice I have a window glazed with two panes of orange glass, to which is added a sheet of white ground glass. Over this runs on rollers a shutter of ruby glass. When I am changing plates, or when the plate is naked, I use the shutter; but after the developer has begun its work I roll back the ruby glass, and then have almost as good a light as when collodion was used.

THE STUDIO OF THE FUTURE will probably have no sloping roof. It is better to abstain from giving advice not based on experience, but if I had to build another studio it would take the form of a square room 26 feet to 30 feet square, 14 feet high, the north side glazed from the top to within 4 feet 6 inches of the ground. This is the simplest possible form, and I believe there would be plenty of light, and that every kind of indoor effect could be got in this room, besides which several difficulties would be avoided. There would be no more fear of the weather; hail and snow may do their worst without doing any damage; and the blinds, being upright, would work with ease.*

To conclude this part of my subject, I give a plan of the studio I have suggested and its accompanying rooms, which can be easily modified to suit different situations, and a section of the studio, showing the angle of the glass at 62° 30'.

---

* Since the first edition of this book was published I have heard of several studios built on this principle, and found to be most successful.

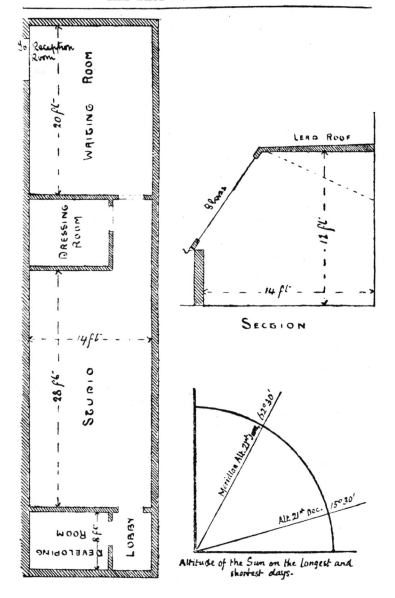

SECTION

Altitude of the Sun on the longest and shortest days.

CHAPTER III.

BACKGROUNDS.

DOUBTLESS, the backgrounds used by photographers have very much improved during the last half-dozen years, but there is still a great deal that wants further improvement. For years writers in the English Photographic Journals preached their little sermons on the fearful things that even photographers of taste were constrained to use, and tried to win over our manufacturers to something more gentle in design, and light, and shade; but it was left for an American to supply the demand, and that the demand for something better was great, is shown by the number of Seavey's backgrounds now used—and pirated. There is a mournful satisfaction in knowing that our background makers can imitate others, if they cannot give us anything original, or indeed useable, of their own.

This refers to pictorial backgrounds; but before I go further I should like to say a word or two on backgrounds in general.

It has been considered by many great artists that the background is not the least important and difficult part of the picture. The proper use of a background is to give relief to the figure, and breadth to the general effect. As we have only a flat surface on which we can suggest the roundness and solidity of nature, we must resort to artifice in the arrangement of the light and shade, to enable us to approach, as near as may be, to a proper expression of nature, and to do this the background gives us the greatest facilities.

In a portrait, the head should be the first attraction, and everything should be subordinate to this part of the picture. In the background especially, by the use of proper lights and shade, and gradations, the head can be much assisted. In some photographic portraits the head is the last thing the spectator is made to think of. The picture often consists of a mass of small details, including a great display of gaudy furniture, and loud curtains and carpets, with the figure as an accessory, and the head apparently an after-thought. Occasionally, the confusion is worse confounded by the addition of plants, such as imitation palms and ferns, and other dead vegetables, sprawling over the scene. Some of these things are all very well in their way, if properly managed, but the portrait should not be sacrificed to them. In a recent exhibition there was a wonderful portrait of a lady in evening dress. The picture was large, the photography was perfect, the chiaroscuro brilliant and broad, but the lady was so embedded in potted plants that your first impression was that she would break some crockery if she moved.

It should be taken as a rule that if you want to give dignity and importance to the figure, you cannot do it by smothering it in small details. Concentration and repose cannot live in the midst of loud and startling effects.

The majority of the best portraits, by the best masters, have no background which strikes the eye, the figure merely being relieved by light and shade, or a variety of broken tints. One of the finest portraits in the world—the Gevartius of Vandyck in the National Gallery—has such a background, and so have hundreds more of the best portraits the world possesses. A background of one uniform tint, unbroken by light and shade, or effect of atmosphere, has an unsatisfactory effect, making the figure appear inlaid, and cutting hard against the background.

Such an effect is often present, and is decidedly unpleasant, in the otherwise noble portraits by Holbein.

For a certain class of photographic portraits, however, the plain background, especially if it be skilfully contrived by variations of light and shade to relieve the figure, will always be most satisfactory. In such cases the sole object of the background is to be as unobtrusive as possible in itself, and to contribute, as far as possible, to give relief and force to the portrait.

In early photographs it will be noticed that the background is nearly always quite plain, without any attempt at gradation. This was probably not so much for want of knowledge in the operator, as from a desire to show his skill. In those days of iodized collodion, it was not an easy matter to produce a picture undisfigured by specks, pinholes, comets, oyster-shell markings, and other of the thousand delights common to the wet process, and the "pride of the workshop" had to be shown in plain, flat spaces, unsullied by any of these defects. But artistic taste in time revolted against blank walls—

> " A wall so blank, my shadow I thank
> For sometimes falling there."

Then came in a desire for gradation, but the means of attaining it were not found to be easy; no background painters existed who would undertake to paint a graduated background, and for want of them many contrivances were suggested for casting shadows. One of the best of these was a simple arrangement of curtains at the side, from which the light came, and a screen over the top of the background, so arranged to move up and down that the shadow could be raised or lowered. The object of most of these contrivances was to throw a shade on the background, melting into a mass of light, which could be so used as to relieve the shadowed side of the head with light, and the lighted side with dark. This arrangement gives great force and richness to the work, and if the gradation is well managed, the head is thrown into strong relief.

Adam Salomon, the famous photographer and sculptor, always laid much stress on the gradation of the background, and was a prolific inventor of contrivances for attaining this object, the most ingenious of which was the alcove background, a sketch and description of which may be interesting, if not useful. For amateurs who take portraits in the open air, the combination of a method of controlling the lighting in connection with the background possesses a distinct advantage.

The structure consists of a semi-circular background, with

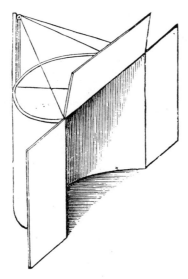

canopy and wings capable of ready arrangement, so as to control the light either on the model or the background. The diagram will help to make the further description clear. The curved background is about 8 feet high and 10 feet wide at the diameter of the circle. Hinged on each side are movable wings, about 4 feet wide, and a canopy, of a similar character and width, is hinged to the top in front. Behind this projecting front canopy is a covering to the curved part of the background; this consists of two halves, hinged in the centre. Attached to the background is an upright, terminating in a series of loops or pulleys. Through these pass cords to work the canopies. The wings and canopy are light frames covered with thin white muslin, transmitting some light, but arresting or breaking up direct rays of sunlight. The background is on castors, so as to be easily movable, and is papered with salmon-coloured paper. Light grey would answer equally well. The size and proportions might be altered to suit circumstances.

To illustrate its working, we will suppose it to be placed in the open air, but it would do equally well in a studio. The sitter is placed in the centre of the circle, of which the curve forms half. We will suppose the front canopy is down, and the wings just so much closed as to form a rectangular opening to the alcove. A soft, diffused light now surrounds the figure. A slight elevation of the canopy at once admits a portion of direct light. In like manner the proportion of side light is modified in any degree by the opening and shutting of the wings. The back canopies also admit light, if desired, when lifted. It will be seen, on a little examination, that almost any amount of light, from any direction, can be allowed to reach the sitter, the means of controlling its direction on him being the most simple and easily managed; and it will be found in practice that however the sitter is lighted, he has gradation of light and shade behind him.

It is fortunate that complicated structures of this kind are no longer needed in the studio. Methods of painting backgrounds are so much improved that most delicate gradations can now be produced on flat surfaces. The illustration is taken from backgrounds I have now in use. The one behind is a light background gradated towards the lower part. This is very useful for vignettes, and when a light background is required. The other is a gradated background to be used with the light coming from the dark side. This produces the effect already mentioned of the shadowed side of the head relieved by light, and the lighted side by dark. A reverse of this should be supplied for use at the opposite end of the room, where the sitter is lighted from the other side. This illustration gives me an opportunity of mentioning a stand for backgrounds I have found very convenient. The backgrounds are stretched on stout frames 8 feet high by 6 feet 6 inches wide. Two of them are placed back to back, and stands

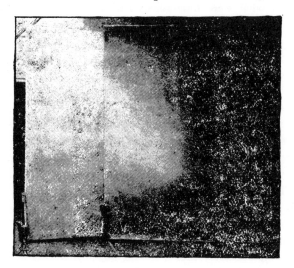

running on good castors screwed to the sides, as shown in the sketch. These backgrounds can be rolled to any part of the studio with the greatest ease, and thus the operator is enabled to place his sitter in any part of the room. Two or more extra backgrounds can be attached to the same stand if they are hinged to the background already fixed, so that they open like the leaves of a book. Care should be taken that they open towards the wall, so as not to obstruct the light when the inner backgrounds are being used.

There are many cases, however, in which a plain background unrelieved by design or accessory will give a meagre and unsatisfactory effect; in most full-length pictures, for instance. To meet this want, pictorial backgrounds were introduced, both of interior and out-door scenes. It is often desirable, also, especially where children are the subjects, and when out-door costume is worn by the sitter, to make up the picture with a pictorial background and foreground accessories.

Everything possible in the way of bad taste has been perpetrated in what were humorously called pictorial backgrounds. It would be useless to point out minutely the kind of thing I allude to. The palatial column and curtain, so suitable for the middle-class citizen; the raging sea and profile rocks, with a carpet on the sands to save the feet of the delicate young lady out in the storm in an evening dress; the pasteboard terrace and distant mole-hills, with fountains squirting out of the sitter's head—they are still to be seen in the albums of those who keep the portraits of twenty years ago; they have not all faded. But we have changed all that. Background painters now pay some attention to possibility and pictorial effect; but they also find that, if they are to obtain the greatest pictorial effect, and if justice is to be done to the portrait, that the background must be, to some extent, conventional. By conventional, I mean that it must not have the full force of nature, but must take a subordinate position; that it should not have all the detail, nor all the force of light and shade of nature; that, in short, while its forms are based on those of nature, it should be such a mass of light and shade as will support the figure without distracting the eye from the head. At the same time, there should be no violent disregard of nature; there should be a general truth, if not a particular one. If the trees have not all their leaves, they should look as if they had been drawn from nature. The distant mountains should look distant. The horizon—ah! there is the difficulty. Where should the horizon be?

There has been, perhaps, more discussion on the position of the horizon in a landscape background than on any other technical detail occurring on the art side of photography. Shall we keep to stern, uncompromising truth, or, for the sake of pictorial effect, shall we depart from the truth of nature? Shall we, as a literal art like photography suggests, keep to absolute fact, or shall we, like Reynolds, Gainsborough, Titian, and many another great portrait painter, depart from fact for the sake of making a better picture? Shall we, in short, give up pictorial effect for the sake of that literal truth which has been described as so praiseworthy—and so intolerable?

The horizon, in nature, is always as high as the eye of the observer. In photography the lens is practically the eye of the observer. If the lens is on a level with the head of the sitter, then the horizon would come behind the head, and if at all defined would interfere with the effect. If the camera were lower than the head, then the horizon would also be low. Many of the great painters wilfully ignored this law of nature, and painted their backgrounds all clouds, with a few inches of ground seldom reaching above the knee. This seems to me to be a matter that may be compromised or evaded. If the camera is placed opposite the breast of a standing figure, then the horizon may be below the shoulders, and leave the head clear against the sky. But when a thing is doubtful, it is better to let it alone altogether. It may be also well to remember that it is never good to push principle to excess, and there may be occasions when the artist would be justified in straining the exact truth, especially on such a disputed point as our present one. There should be a sufficient choice of subjects for backgrounds without any horizon whatever. In a background there should be no false lines. The sitter and distance should be under the same conditions of perspective as well as light and shade.

The photographer is much more restricted, both in resource and aim, than the painter in the management of his background.

Fuseli says : " By the choice and scenery of the background we are frequently enabled to judge how far a painter entered into his subject, whether he understood its nature, to what class it belonged, what impression it was capable of making, what passion it was calculated to arouse; the sedate, the solemn, the severe, the awful, the terrible, the sublime, the placid, the solitary, the pleasing, the gay, are stamped by it. Sometimes it ought to be negative, entirely subordinate, receding or shrinking into itself; sometimes more positive : it acts, invigorates, assists the subject. A subject in itself bordering on the common, may become sublime or pathetic by the background alone ; and a sublime or pathetic one may become trivial and uninteresting by it." The range of effect here indicated far transcends anything possible to the photographer. Nevertheless, he may at times give character to his pictures by the selection of characteristic backgrounds and accessories. But it is clear that the use of such accessories can only become the exception, and not the rule, as by far the greater majority of portraits do not admit of any such aid from characterisation. It is manifest, moreover, that the photographer cannot, like the painter, prepare a background of different and characteristic design for each picture. If, then, he is under the necessity of using the same or similar backgrounds for all ranks and conditions of men—the peer and peasant alike—they must of necessity be sufficiently devoid of special character to suit any without incongruity.

CHAPTER IV.

ACCESSORIES.

Accessories have given thoughtful portraitists more trouble than any other part of their art connected with picture-making. Many have taken refuge in those Protean machines which are "everything by turns, and nothing long," but have not been able to hide from themselves that a piece of furniture that could be turned into a score of absurd incongruities at will was a sham, and therefore unworthy of the truthful art. As a rule, everything that is made purposely for studio use smacks of the studio, and proclaims itself as a make-up. Of course, in saying this, I do not object to making-up, or anything that will aid in producing a picture, for what is art, after all, *but* make-up? What I do object to is, that the art should be made too palpable. Any furniture that is made for the studio, and is seen nowhere else, is objectionable. A chair, for instance, that is made for a figure to lean on, and looks like it; a sham piano, painted a dull grey, so that it may "take" well; sham windows and *papier maché* chimney pieces; the posing chair that is half a couch; the elaborately carved table—all these are bad. Just such furniture as is found in the houses of ordinary reasonable beings is what is wanted, and as much variety of this as you like.

It was once the fashion to fill the studio with old carved oak furniture from Wardour Street, and a photographer would take a good deal of trouble to show off his ornate table at the risk of detracting from the effect of the head of the portrait. He had the excuse for using this stuff, that the ordinary furniture of the day was about as ugly as it could be made. There is no such excuse now. The art of design has made giant strides during the last twenty years, and in no department is this more conspicuous than in furniture.

The once much-abused curtain may be used, but not in the old way. The column is now banished; and the heavy rep material tied up in ugly folds, with a very pronounced cord and tassel following the lines of the figure instead of contrasting it, can no longer be allowed. There is now a great variety of beautiful materials within easy reach of the photographer, one of the best of which is Madras muslin. This is a thin fabric that easily falls into graceful folds, and the designs are in the very best taste. One of these curtains, tastefully arranged on a screen, gives light to a background that was in danger of being too plain and dull, while the lines can be adapted so as to agree with the composition of the figure. I have mentioned a screen. A screen is of great service in a studio. A three or four-leaf folding Japanese screen is perhaps the best. It can be put to a variety of uses in making up backgrounds, and is useful for other purposes.

There is great virtue in variety. If the photographer would make up his mind never to take two pictures alike, he would strengthen his inventive powers, make his show frames more attractive, and life more interesting to him. The monotony of making all men and women lean on the same chair, in the same position, and photographing them one after another, from week's end to week's end, must be dreadful. The continual use even of a good thing is objectionable. Who is not weary of the eternal rustic stile, evidently quite new from the workshop, and, like the Irish gate, without any hedge or fence on either side, so that you must make believe almost as much as Dick Swiveller's Marchioness, if you want to persuade yourself there is no other way to the village than over the bars? Now a stile in itself is a very picturesque thing, so also may be a wicket gate, but the way they are, as a rule, made and used, seems to proclaim with a grin that there is no deception. Even if the stile was perfect in its way, it would become very tiresome from constant use. The same remarks apply to the ship's mast and the swing, both good of their kind, when used occasionally and in season, but not when they are pressed into service for all purposes against nature and art.

In deprecating palpably made-up articles, I am far from objecting to properly made aids to posing, such as balconies and balustrades ; occasionally such things add much, for instance, to the portrait of a lady in walking dress, or to a group of children in outdoor costume ; but to be unobjectionable, they should be kept subdued, and used sparingly. These accessories are usually sent out from the manufactory painted one uniform drab colour. It would be easy to paint them to look old and weather-stained.

For seaside studios a real boat—or half a one, if you must economise space—is a valuable accessory, and is much better than the sham, profile article which is often used, and always speaks for itself. I have seen the bows of a real old boat used with great effect, and it was found to be very suggestive of poses. A bit of old rope, some netting, pebbles, crab baskets, and other objects of the seaside, also aided in the realistic effect.

Besides the ordinary furniture, there are a number of other things that are necessary for the use of the portraitist. Among others I find a small platform, standing about 16 inches from the ground, and measuring about 4 feet square, very useful in posing children. There is always a difficulty in getting down to them when they are placed on the floor. Specially short head-rests have to be used, and the camera lowered to an inconvenient extent. If the platform is made to fold in the middle, with a leg to pull out to support the leaf, as is seen in some tables, it takes very little room. With some well-made rocks of different sizes, and bits of hay on this platform, very natural portraits of children can easily be arranged. Among the smaller articles that should be at hand, there should be a good supply of baskets of various shapes, and vases with flowers, natural by preference, but well-made artificial ones if the real ones cannot be got. Two or three fans will be found useful, and above all there should be a grand collection of toys for the children, from the squeaking india-rubber baby up to the boyish hoop and the more manly cricket bat, not forgetting the tennis racquet. The most beautiful thing about the most beautiful child is nearly always the expression, and the photographer can only hope to make the best of the little sitter by descending down to the level of the child. A photographer who cannot play with toys, and enjoy the game, too, while he is about it, ought not to try to take children. Toys specially made to attract the attention of children should be at hand. A loud ticking watch is always useful, so also is a musical box; and a good deal can be done with the india-rubber toys which give, on squeezing, that plaintive expression to their feelings so dear to childhood.

REFLECTING SCREENS.—As a rule, for ordinary portraiture, no reflected light, other than the natural reflection from the grey paper wall, will be necessary, but there are occasions when a reflector may be useful. It sometimes happens, in taking shadow pictures, that it is difficult to introduce a weakened light to relieve the shaded side, and secure the discrimination of forms and textures. All broad, strong masses of shadow should be broken up, or rather light should be let into them; for this purpose nothing is better than a screen 4 or 5 feet square, papered white and mounted on a stand; or one of the leaves of an ordinary folding screen may be papered for the purpose.

Many elaborate contrivances have been invented or suggested for casting reflections, but they take up more space and give more trouble than they are worth. One of the simplest and most effective reflectors, other than a plain screen, was suggested by Adam Salomon. In describing his reflector, he says:— " The reflected lights ought to be as much under the operator's control as the direct light, and a strong reflected light, perfectly under control, may often possess all the value of direct light. In the little contrivance shown in the diagram I have

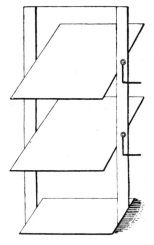

the most perfect control over the reflected lights, which may be thrown in any direction, up or down, or nearly all round the figure. It consists of a simple, upright framework of wood, about 6 feet high and 3 feet wide, with a couple of reflectors 3 feet square, each swinging on its axis in the framework, and moved by the handles into any position. One side of each reflector is painted white, and the other side is covered with polished tin, the latter to give the strongest reflection when required. The frame can be placed in almost any position towards the shadowed side of the model, and the two reflectors can be made to throw light on any portion of the shadowed side. The use and the value of the contrivance will be apparent without many words. It may or may not be new, but I have not seen one before, and it is, at any rate, sufficiently valuable, although trifling, to induce me to offer it to my English friends."

Finally, every accessory, from the steps of Haddon Hall to the rattle and the ball, should have its own place, so that it can be used at once without any trouble or loss of time.*

---

* Lest it be said that I have omitted to mention the principal object in the studio—the camera—I may as well say here that the optical and chemical side of photography does not enter into my plan. That part of the subject is exhaustively treated by Capt. Abney in his "Handy Books."

CHAPTER V.

LIGHTING THE SITTER.

As the succeeding chapters on Posing will have little or nothing
to do with light and shade, a few words on the mechanical
means of producing and regulating light and shade on the sitter
by the use of blinds, screens and reflectors, may not be out of
place as an introduction.

The first aim of the student in lighting a head—leaving out
of the question, for the moment, what may be called "fancy"
lighting, such as Rembrandts—should be to get roundness and
relief, to obtain gradation, and to avoid patches of black and
white; to so light the head that beauties are made prominent
and defects hidden. Or, as Mr. Mayall once summed up the
objects of lighting: "To render age less garrulous; make beauty
more lovely; to impart an expression of intelligence where
nature has not been over bountiful; to light up the intellect,
and to impart the quality of power in those heads on which she
has lavished her most precious gifts; in short, to present human
nature in its best form, by aid of a camera and a properly-lighted
room." The general chiaroscuro of a picture will not be discussed here, as I have gone fully into the subject in a former
work.*

---

* "Pictorial Effect in Photography." Published by Piper and Carter.

I will suppose that the student is working in a studio such as that described in Chapter II. When he has learnt what to get and how to get it in this form of studio, he will be able to apply his knowledge in other studios.

In his first serious studies in lighting, I should recommend the student to use a life-sized plaster cast. It has been objected that this will not yield the same results as studying effects on the human subject, because one is simple, the other complex. This is just the reason why I recommend the plaster bust to the young student; he should commence his studies under simple conditions, avoiding the complex until he has quite mastered the more simple ones. Whilst studying the effects of light on a white or grey bust, there is no fear of tiring the model, therefore no cause for hurry; no disturbing influence of colour ; he sees exactly the effect of light in producing high lights, reflected lights, and shadows in his picture. Having once learned to produce and recognise on the bust satisfactory and pictorial effects of light and shade, he will soon learn to apply what he has learned to the lighting of the living model.

To make my remarks as clear as possible, I give a diagram of the glazed part of the roof of the studio, showing the blinds.

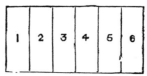

In most studios of this form the spaces occupied by blinds 1 and 6 are usually solidly-constructed roofs, but I prefer to let the glass run from end to end, as it is of use to the photographer in getting pictures lighted from the back. Besides, too much glass can easily be modified by blinds; too little does not admit of such a remedy. The six blinds in a studio 28 feet long, would each be 4 feet 8 inches wide; if the studio be of a shorter length, I should prefer to reduce the width of blinds 2, 3, 4, and 5, and keep 1 and 6 of the full width of from 4 feet 8 inches to 5 feet.

Blinds 1 and 6 should be of some black material, and the others of white, or the grey striped material called "Union." The whole of them should run on rollers at the top, pulled up easily by weights or springs. The blinds should always be in good order, and ready to obey the least touch of the operator. There should be another black blind, pulling up from the eaves and doubling blinds 3 and 4. The use of this blind will be seen further on.

The subject of lighting the sitter has been often treated, and treated as it only can be, in general terms. The special lighting of each sitter is, after all, a question which can only be solved by the operator when he has that sitter before him. He must see that the light and shade fall so as to produce the most agreeable effect before he exposes his plate, and with the capacity of seeing this, the power of modifying it is usually accompanied. I can only tell him what to look for generally, and the influence of the blinds in producing the desired effect.

As a general principle, a high side-light, a little in advance of the sitter, is the most important direct light; excess of vertical light is, in most cases, to be avoided; nevertheless, it may be useful at times in giving force and brilliancy to flat, commonplace faces, which in themselves possess very little relief. For example, I think I should use a good deal of vertical light in taking the portrait of a Chinaman. On the other hand, where the sitter has heavy brows, sunken eyes, or prominent features, the least possible vertical light should be employed, or these features will look more marked and heavy. With such faces the side-light, well in advance of the sitter, will give the most soft and harmonious effect without risk of flatness. The top front light will generally serve to illumine sufficiently the shadowed side of the face without the use of reflecting screens other than the natural reflection from the grey paper of the wall.

Reflecting screens will, however, under·certain circumstances, be found useful. As a rule, a mild, soft light is what is required. Strong illumination produces lights and shadows of great intensity, giving black and white pictures; and the glare of brilliant light interferes with the expression of the sitter.

There are other influences besides the amount of space through which light is admitted. The aspect of the day, the period of the year, the quality of the light, the situation of the studio, whether in town or country, at the top of the house or on the ground; even the quality of the plate, for a very sensitive plate seems to require a greater contrast of light and shade than a slow one.

All these things prevent anything like the establishment of fixed rules for lighting. There is no patent way to "fix your light."

The true test of good lighting is roundness. This can only be got by securing delicacy in the half-tones; there should be no broad patches of black and white, but gradation everywhere. The operator must educate himself to *see* these half tones, and he must see them in the model, without the trouble and delay of looking at the ground glass, or taking and printing a negative. Get the right effect in nature, and the rest will follow—

"As the sitter's lighted, so's the picture drawn."

Having stated briefly what is required, let us walk into the studio, and try to reduce our theories to practice.

We will begin by placing the bust on a table at the east end, about 3 feet from the background, and place ourselves in the middle of the room where the camera would stand. The blinds are all drawn down, and for the purposes of the lesson, we will suppose the south wall to be too dark to act as a reflector.

The effect ought now to be, not darkness, but a dull light of no photographic use. The model looks moderately round, but without high-lights or details in the shadows.

Pull up No. 2 blind all the way. You will find that the light is too vertical, and that the shadows under the eyebrows are dark and heavy. Pull down the blind half-way. The black vertical shadows are softened. The high-lights on the forehead and nose appear. There is enough light, although the space opened is under 6 feet by 5 feet, to get a negative with a moderate exposure, but the shadowed side of the face is too dark and without transparency. Place a grey reflecting screen on the shadowed side, and the shadows will look softer, and the reflected light will show detail. The dark side, however, is still too dark for a delicately lighted head. There are several ways of altering this. One would be to replace the grey screen with a white one, but there is danger in this of throwing a light into the eye, giving a strange, blind effect. The best way of lighting the dark side is to pull up No. 3 to the top, and if this is not sufficient, to raise No. 6. If this again is not sufficient— and it is not in some phases of the light, such as when a luminous white cloud is passing—then it would be advisable to

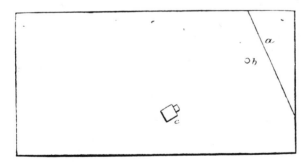

work diagonally, as shown in the diagram. *a* is the background, *b* the sitter, *c* the camera.

Thus far, by way of lesson; but if the operator wants to have his room so arranged that he need seldom think of his lighting or his blinds, except for fancy lighting, let him arrange his skylight as follows :—

Blinds No. 1 and 6 black.

No. 2 and 5 half up.

No. 3 and 4 ground glass or tissue paper; the blinds up.

The wall to be papered with a light grey diaper.

It will be found that, with this arrangement, a head placed 3 or 4 feet from either background will be full of subtle gradations, with sparkling high-lights and sharp touches of dark. It would be well also to note, with this lighting, the different effects on the head as it advances more towards the centre of the studio. Very soft effects are to be got by placing the sitter about 6 feet from the end backgrounds. The photographer should study the light in every part of his room.

I have said nothing of the difference of effect on a full face and a profile. It will be found that a flatter light than that used for a full or three-quarter will be better for a side face.

Fancy Lighting.—Very picturesque effects are to be got by the various modes of lighting the sitter which have gradually come under the designation of what is now called Fancy Lighting. Of these the Rembrandt effect obtains the most favour. The Rembrandt portrait is usually a head, more or less in profile, lighted from behind and the side, and as unlike anything Rembrandt ever painted as possible. I have always objected to this title for these shadow pictures, but the name sticks, and I accept it.

To light a Rembrandt, place the sitter under the junction of blinds 2 and 3, but rather more under 3. Pull up No. 2 half-way. Pull down 3 and 4, and if this does not make the shadowed side dark enough, there should be another black blind working under and supplementing 3 and 4, rolling up at the bottom and working upwards, but not quite to the top. Turn the head of the sitter in profile towards the light. With this arrangement it will be found that there is a bright light down the edge of the nose, and on part of the cheek. The shadowed side is probably too black; anyway, it may be taken as a rule that shadow, however dark it may be wanted, is always better for some reflected light to make out the forms, and give transparency. This can be done by the use of a reflecting screen, or blind No. 4 may be drawn up to the top, letting a little light on the dark side, over the edge of the black blind, which, it will be remembered, does not reach to the top. The shadow can also be modified by gradually withdrawing the black blind, and allowing weak light to get through the white or grey blinds, Nos. 3 and 4.

A good effect is also to be got by turning the sitter's face quite away from the light, looking to the wall; in this case the profile is entirely in shadow, and should have a light background. I have entered further into this subject in the next chapter.

The operator should occupy his leisure time in trying experiments in lighting, and in trying to get away from the hum-drum effects he is compelled to produce in the ordinary round of daily portraiture, recollecting, however, that the illumination should be adapted to the sex, age, and physiognomical peculiarities of the sitter—to bring out beauties, and to hide defects.

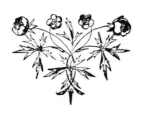

CHAPTER VI.

POSING AND THE MANAGEMENT OF THE SITTER.
THE HEAD.

In the following chapters I hope to give some general ideas on posing sitters for portraiture, suitable for the requirements of the professional photographer—not, I trust, without being of some use to the amateur. I do not intend to confine myself to the ornamental and elaborate, but shall prefer to give such simple advice as, in my opinion, is calculated to be of most use in ordinary studio practice. Much of it, perhaps, will seem too elementary for the skilled photographer, but I trust that here and there may crop up ideas worthy of the attention of even the most experienced operator. In doing this, I protest against the enervating practice of giving a set of poses for the imitation of those idle and thoughtless operators who do not try to think for themselves and adapt their ideas to their subjects, but who place their sitters, no matter how unsuitable it may be to them, in the same position day after day, as if the posing chair was a sort of Procrustean bed on which everybody must be cut to the same size and shape and form, and brought to that state of imbecile appearance to which photography is popularly supposed to reduce its victims. A recent writer on composition has some forcible remarks on this point. He says : " Our subjects and our treatment of them must be emphatically our own ; but nevertheless, every student of art owes it to himself to get what help he can from the study of the works of the great painters who have gone before. His object should be to notice not only how natural appearances have been modified—or, as it is technically called, treated—by painters of acknowledged fame, but also why this was done. No painter who has in him any spark of originality will directly repeat any effect that has already been painted; but an earnest student can only benefit himself by trying in a measure to look at nature from the point of view of the masters of his art."

For the purpose of these lessons, portraiture may be divided into different classes, such as the head, the three-quarter, the full-length, the seated, the standing, the group, &c. Of all this variety the head is, perhaps, the most important, for nine-tenths of the portraits taken in ordinary studios—excluding the lower class and "the beach"—consist of heads taken under different names, as the Vignette, the Berlin, the Medallion, the Rembrandt. Now it might be thought that nothing could be simpler or easier than to pose a head, and that there was very little to say on the subject; but if we are to judge by the majority of specimens, we see that the art of setting a head properly on its shoulders is not given to all men, and the results suggest the notion that their victims were first hanged—*sus. per col.*—and then, instead of being "drawn," according to the old sentence, had been photographed. This broken-necked effect is more visible in Rembrandts than in the other forms mentioned, although they are not absent from Vignettes and Medallions. The reason why it is more apparent in Rembrandts, probably, is, that this kind of picture is commonly taken in profile, and the strain to turn the head sufficiently makes it lean towards the camera. On the next page is an illustration. You have only to add a rope to make the thing complete.

The eye, also, in these shadow portraits, nearly always seems to be afraid of looking straight—the shy, half-frightened, and wholly-deceitful glance of the eye in most of these pictures, suggesting that none but the very worst characters ever had their portraits done in this style. Both these very grave faults are easily avoided. The inclination of the head towards the camera is caused chiefly, as I have said, by the strain in turning to a side view of the face when the body is in full front view. If the figure were turned to a three-quarter view towards the light, the strain would be lessened, and if the head still leans over too much, a very slight movement of the head by the photographer would set it upright. But I must take the

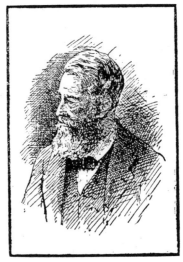

opportunity that here presents itself of saying that the less the operator handles his sitter, the better. It worries him, and oftener tends, except in very skilled hands, to stiffen the figure rather than add to its grace.

The defect in the eye, just mentioned, is caused entirely by having the light too low down, so that the sitter, if he looks straight, is dazzled, and has to look aside. There is no reason whatever why there should be any light in a studio lower than

5 feet from the ground. A studio of the following section answers every purpose, and, as the solid walls are not less than 4 feet 6 inches high, the eye of the sitter for a Rembrandt portrait may be looking at a pleasant picture instead of a glaring light.

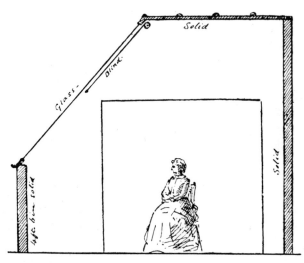

There is, apparently, very little glass used here, but it will be found quite enough. And if a space of clear glass, measuring 5 feet by 4 feet, just behind and to the side of the sitter, be used, the rest of the roof may be obscured, or semi-obscured, leaving the possibility, however, of letting in a little reflected light on the shadowed side of the head. The shadow pictures are very much improved if some gradation of light and shade can be obtained in the background, and fine effects can be got by turning the face from the light, and bringing it out dark against a light background.

The head-rest is now seldom used, and is chiefly famous for the unmeasured abuse it met with from the ungrateful sitters for whose benefit it was invented, and is still, in good hands, a great aid in posing. Objectors never stop to think that it is not the instrument that is in fault, but the clumsy users of it. I notice in my own practice that the complaints against the rest are not so frequent as they were once upon a time, and if a sitter objects to the rest, I feel certain that he has been badly treated, and had an awful experience with some other photographer, and make it a point of honour to induce him not only to submit to, but to enjoy it.

The rest should not be treated as an instrument to keep the sitter still, but as a posing machine. One of the most objectionable things you can do to a sitter is to insist on his being still. You of course want him to be quiet while the exposure is going on, but this should result from your general treatment of him, rather than any preconceived notion he may have brought with him. He should be so managed that sufficient stillness is a natural result. During the few seconds' exposure that is all now necessary, a slight touch of the rest, properly applied, is enough to secure steadiness, but its great use is in making slight variations of the pose—of which more hereafter—and the confidence it gives the sitter that he is not going to spoil your plate by moving. On the other hand, if you dispense with the rest, the sitter makes a desperate struggle to keep still, and *looks like it*. Now the portrait of a gentleman, with an expression of firm determination to keep steady, as if rigidity was the one absorbing passion of his life, is not a pleasant object to contemplate.

The rest should be a comfort instead of a nuisance. It should be adjusted to the head, and not the head to the rest. It should never be applied until everything else is ready. A sitter should never have time to feel how ridiculous he looks, and the longer he is fixed to the rest, the more this feeling obtrudes itself. The plate should be exposed as quickly as possible after the rest is placed. If a slight alteration strikes you as a possible advantage, it is better to give it up than disturb the sitter at this moment; but if there is anything gravely wrong in the pose or dress, it is better to begin all over again.

The rest should be understood to be, and used as, a delicate support to the head and figure, not a rigid fixture against which the figure is to lean. As used in most studios, it is a great deal too heavy. There is no occasion whatever for the cumbrous iron supports so often employed. For ordinary portraiture I prefer a light, simple rest, without any complications—one that can be easily carried about after the sitter without trouble. I have no fixed place for the sitter in my studio, but place him in any part, just as the fancy strikes me, and it is here I find a light rest of so much use. A perfect rest has yet to be made. It must be moderately light and portable, and very simple. The complicated movements of the ordinary machines, often with chairs attached, are worse than useless, and very confusing.

The head-rest is not exclusively a photographer's tool; it is sometimes used by sculptors. The following curious extract from Leslie's "Autobiographical Recollections" will show that Chantrey not only used one of these machines, but also employed the best substitute for our art the science of his time would afford. Had he lived in our day, he would never have commenced a bust until he had obtained a satisfactory photograph of his sitter for his guidance.

"July 31st, 1836.—In the evening I went to Mr. Dunlop's. Mr. Dunlop had been sitting to Chantrey, who fixed the back of his head in a wooden machine, to keep him perfectly still, and then drew with a cameralucida the profile and front face of the size of life. He afterwards gave a little light and shade to the drawings, and said, ' I shall not require you to sit still after this.' He said, ' I always determine in my own mind the expression to be given, and unless I can see the face distinctly, and with that expression when I close my eyes, I can do nothing. If I can, I can often make the face more like in the absence of the sitter than in his presence.' "

E

CHAPTER VII.

POSING AND THE MANAGEMENT OF THE SITTER.
THE HEAD VIGNETTE.

In the last chapter I left my man hanging, while I went off
into a digression on studios and head-rests, turning him, indeed
—as well as my chapter—into a " subject " quite other than
that intended. This is bad art. A subject should never be
left suspended. Years ago there was published a series of portraits of a famous actress as she appeared reciting Tennyson's
sensational " Charge of the Light Brigade," a poem utterly
unworthy of the great poet's genius, but which, however, still
finds listeners, if not readers. There were seven poses in all,
and the last of the series left the lady with arms extended in
the very ecstacy of declamation ; to make the series complete,
and finish artistically, the photographer should have added
another picture with arms down, and left her in repose.

We will continue the consideration of how a head ought to be
treated.

The first thing to decide when you see your sitter should be :
" Which side of his face will make the best picture ? " This
consideration seldom gives an experienced operator any trouble.
To one who is in the habit of observing, the sides of every face
differ so much, and in such a definite manner, that a glance is
all that is necessary to settle the question ; but the young

photographer will want to know how to select, and have some rule for the selection.

If you will look critically at a full face (or the photograph of a full face would be better, as it would enable you to measure), you will find that the eyes are not level—one is higher than the other. This is almost invariable, and is one of the peculiar instances in which nature insists on variety even where uniformity would seem to be proper. If you take a photograph of the face in a three-quarter position, with the eye that is highest away from you, the unevenness will be still more visible; but if you take the other side of the face, and have

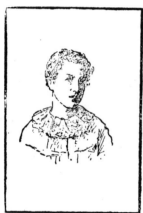 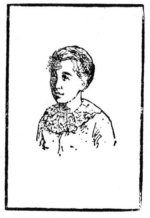

the highest eye nearest to the camera, the lower eye will seem to fall away naturally, through the effect of perspective. The same facts apply to the nose, sometimes in a very marked degree; and it fortunately happens, in nine cases out of ten, that the eyes and nose agree as to which is the best side of the face. When they disagree, the portrait is seldom satisfactory. The two illustrations are taken from different sides of the same face, and show which side should have been taken. In the one to the right the nose looks broken, and the eyes out of line; in the other these defects are not seen.

I keep an illustrated catalogue of all the portraits I take, and on looking through several volumes, I found confirmed a very curious idea that was stated in a "Note" in the PHOTOGRAPHIC NEWS. I found that about four out of five of the portraits were taken looking to the right, showing that I had in these instances chosen the left side as the best. Now, as both ends of my studio are equally well lighted, and it is no more trouble to take one side of the face than the other, it follows that, in my judgment, in four out of five cases the left side was the best. If this is correct, the knowledge of it would be of some practical use to those who have to build studios in a confined place, with only one end available, to make it that end on which the left side of the face can be best lighted.

If your sitter is not in a good state to be photographed, and if it does not endanger the loss of him (this is a purely business consideration, which is out of place here), it is much better to postpone the sitting than to risk taking an indifferent portrait. The other day I saw that one of my sitters was not looking his best, and asked him if anything was the matter. "Well," he replied, "I've got a headache that ought to be good enough to split a planet into fragments, but I thought I would keep my appointment." Now, it is a good thing to encourage sitters to be punctual, but I felt it right to send this one away for a day or two. My friend's description of a perfect and complete headache was as good as I had heard until another friend said he had got an effervescing mixture of sunstroke and neuralgia.

A sitter will sometimes want to be taken "naturally." His ideas of being natural—"just as I am, you know"—is to sprawl over the furniture. Perhaps he will put his hands in his pockets, sink low in the chair, and expect you to make a good head and shoulders of him. This is an awkward customer to manage. Possibly the best plan is to recommend him to go to the worst photographer he can find—one of those who advertise themselves loudly as "artists," without knowing the meaning of the word (there are plenty of them in every town), or to the peripatetic on the sands or common, who will let him have his own way entirely, so that he pays his sixpence in advance.

But, given a decent sitter who, for the present purpose, let us say, wants a head and shoulders—what is called a vignette head—the question is, what to do with him.

A conscientious photographer who desires to do his best, and who charges a price that will allow him to forget the cost of his materials, will, in this case, take at least three positions—a full, or nearly full, face; a three-quarter; and, if the face will bear it, a profile, or nearly profile, showing a little of the off eyebrow; but if the side face would be too trying, then the third negative may be devoted to a variation of expression in one of the other positions.

A simple head requires to be properly composed as much as any other kind of picture, and should not be without variety of line and contrast. If, with a full face, the body is also turned full towards the camera, a line drawn down the middle of the picture would divide it into two halves, as nearly corresponding as variety-loving nature will allow; but if the body is turned a little away, and the face to the camera, there will be variety of line suggesting movement and life, especially if the expression can be made to correspond. For a three-quarter face it is better to turn the figure quite in profile, or even showing a little of the back; or the figure may be full and the head turned away; either way will give a lively and agreeable turn to the neck. The same remarks will apply to a profile, except that there must not be too much strain in the neck, so as to pitch the head forwards, as already alluded to in the last chapter.

In a "head," the shoulders should be always nearly level, and the figure upright. It looks awkward to see one shoulder much higher than the other, when the rest of the figure is not shown to account for the position. Some sitters are obstinate about this, and will not sit upright, preferring, as they say, to feel at ease and " natural," as if it were their feelings they wanted photographed, instead of their appearance. The only remedy for a bad case of this kind is to make your subject stand. This usually improves the fall of the shoulders; it is also a sovereign cure for another difficulty. Some sitters, if you ask them to sit upright, will think they are complying with your wishes if they lean back in the chair and stick their chins in the air, for there are people who think they are not upright until they are nearly falling backwards. This leaning back in the chair, added to too much twist to the neck, is the cause of nearly all the broken-necked effects. A good deal can be done with a skilful use of the body-rest; but the best remedy, as I have already said, is to make the subject stand.

The eyes should always *go with the head*. Nothing is more

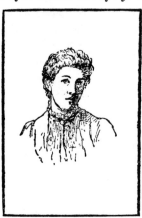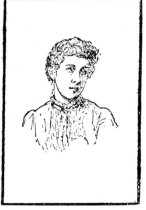

disagreeable than to see an eye looking out of the corner, or twisted across the face. The eyes of a full or nearly full face should look full at the camera; a little above the lens I prefer, if you can trust your sitter not to drop the eye as the cap is removed. If the head is turned to the right, the eye should go as much to the right; if a little more it is no great matter, but it should never come back again, or a shy or frightened look will be given. The second illustration is the same head exactly as the first, as near as I can draw it, with the position of the eyes only altered. The first is constrained and self-conscious, the other easy and natural.

I am not sure that I explain quite clearly what I mean when I say the eyes should go with the head; it would have been better if I had exaggerated the effect I intended to condemn in my illustration. The pose I deprecate is that seen in the portraits by Lely and Kneller, and the painters of their time, who seem to have supposed that the more a figure was twisted, the more graceful it became. In these portraits the figure would be turned to the right, the face to the left, and the eyes back again to the right. Now, if in this pose the eyes had looked in the same direction as the head—or, in other words, to the point to which the head is turning—instead of looking back again, the effect would be natural and graceful, instead of fantastic and artificial. A variation of this twisted posing is presented when the figure and eyes are full, and the face turned away. This does not apply to a pose—often adopted by Vandyck and other great artists—in which the figure is turned slightly away, the face three-quarter or nearly full, and the eyes quite full. In this case I hold that *the eyes go with the head*, because they are both going towards the same point.

Many sitters who look bright and lively when they talk, sink suddenly into the opposite extreme. As they speak the last word their head drops, and a sort of reactionary expression comes on; this expression is as much the result of the drop of the head as the alteration in the features, and must be looked out for and counteracted. If a head-rest is used without any support to the back, this result is almost inevitable. Some photographers use a posing-chair—sometimes called a vignetting-chair—which supports the back; but I prefer to use a back-rest. Indeed, I use this rest constantly, and could not do without it. The use of the rest should be a fine art.

CHAPTER VIII.

POSING AND THE MANAGEMENT OF THE SITTER.
THE THREE-QUARTER LENGTH—MEN.

In the kind of picture we have now under consideration, there is more scope for variety of pose than in those which include the head and shoulders only. Almost every variety of picturesque effect can be brought to bear, both of light and shade and line.

The three-quarter length is generally supposed to include the figure down to the knees, but in treating of it we may fairly include a proportion that takes in somewhat less, and is more nearly a half-length.

For ordinary every-day portraiture of ordinary humanity, no great variety of pose is necessary—or, indeed, admissible. This is especially so as regards the photographic presentation of men. If you will go through a modern exhibition—for example, the Royal Academy—and take a general and comparative survey of all those pictures which used to be catalogued under the title of "portrait of a gentleman," you will find that the variety in the pose is very limited. This is due in a great measure to the restraint that modern dress imposes on the artist. The masculine coat and trousers of to-day do not admit of artistic arrangement, and any attempt to alter them savours of affectation. Adam Salomon's black velvet cloak was very picturesque as arranged by his artistic hands, but it looked out of place on a Manchester merchant or a book-maker. Sôme of our best portrait-painters seem to have given up all hope of varying the position of their sitters, and seat them all, with rare exceptions, in the same chair in endless succession. I do not state this for the photographer's imitation ; he had better always strive for improvement, and not give up all effort as the painters seem to do when they are elected into the Academic body, but as some little comfort for him when his efforts to become original fail.

Photography has done much to teach the painter. There can be no doubt that our art has greatly improved portrait painting. When photographers began to take portraits, portraiture in paint was at its lowest ebb ; it is now at its greatest since the time of Gainsborough and Reynolds. Our art has been especially useful in teaching the painter what to avoid ; it has completely abolished the column and curtain. I don't think this once inevitable background has been seen in the Academy Exhibitions for several years. It has taught him how to give individuality and character. In every portrait painter's work before the introduction of photography, one face was very like another, and it has taught him that conventionality is only to be tolerated in decorative work.

But if there is very little variety open to the operator in his portraits of men, there is one posture that I should like to see entirely discarded, and never used any more. This pose is hallowed by tradition, and sanctified by use, for it has been the one pose of photographers since the morning twilight of the art. It is the pose with which the amateur begins ; with which the professional, however capable of art knowledge, commences ; and with which the incapable spends all his days. I give it on the next page as an example of what to avoid.

Who does not know, who has not been guilty of, this pose, in which the victim appears to be laid out and trussed, little round table and all ? It is all very well, the young photographer will say, to tell me what to avoid—destructive criticism is always easy; but I want to be told what to do. I can only reply by again resorting partly to pointing out what to avoid.

Let us take a portrait. The subject is a gentleman of any age between twenty-five and fifty; he wants a standing portrait. To begin, make him stand in as easy an attitude as possible; don't dictate to him how he shall stand at first, but let him take his own position, and use his suggestion if good; alter it a little if necessary, but don't "mess the figure about." If it does not easily "come," make him walk away and try

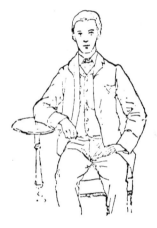

again. It is possible he may have an idea that he ought to be upright when he stands for a picture, and will stand equally on both legs. Now, however strange it may seem, human beings seldom stand on both legs at once, except in their first and second childhood. Infants and very old men *toddle* equally on both feet. Between these ages a person, when standing at ease, rests on one leg, and in walking it is one or other leg alternately that bears the burden. By this means nature gives variety of line, and avoids the uniformity it abhors. In posing a man, strive to get sufficient variety to give picturesqueness. Do not let the head be in exact line with the body; if the figure is turned full, let the face be in three-quarter view; if the figure is slightly turned away, the face may be full or in profile. See that there is variety in the figure; do not let the hands appear as two spots exactly opposite each other on both sides; do not allow uniformity in the furniture and accessories; for instance, if there is a chair on one side of him, it would be better not to have another on the other side. I do not like to speak too definitely, for fear of cramping the operator instead of helping him; and I can quite conceive cases where exactly the reverse of what I have recommended would be exactly what was wanted. If possible, avoid the leaning position—the pedestal and back-of-chair business has been thoroughly overdone. So much are some sitters, who often have their portraits taken, used to it, that they naturally ask for something to lean on.

"It makes me feel so easy and natural," a man will say; but is puzzled when asked if he can ever remember leaning on a pedestal, and looking like the monument of Shakespeare, anywhere but in a photographer's studio. I remember a studio, in the days of the carte-de-visite mania, where the pedestal and head-rest were fixed institutions, and every figure was fitted to them, all with their legs crossed, like Crusaders on their tombs, only upright.

To a seated figure the same suggestion for variety will apply. A man will sometimes think he looks easy when he feels so, and will slouch down in a chair, put his hands in his pockets, shrug up his shoulders, and, putting his foot up over the knee of the other leg, will present the sole of his boot as the principal object in the picture. But it is "not thy sole, but thy soul," as Gratiano says to the Jew, that is wanted in a portrait, and the lounger must be shaken up. Some young men think it looks easy and graceful to sit astride on a chair, and lean their elbows on the back. To me they look awkward and ungraceful in this position, and all I can say about it is, that it is just allowable when it cannot be avoided.

Old men usually make admirable photographs. There is a gravity about old age that seems to suit photography. White hair may be a technical difficulty, but it is to be got over by judicious lighting and manipulation, and difficulty ought to lend a zest to all arts. Old people are usually steady without much effort, and, as a rule, they do not care so much how they look as younger people do, and therefore are free from the self-conscious look that so sadly mars nearly all portraits, whether painted or photographed. Seated positions, in arm-chairs for preference, seem to be most suitable for age.

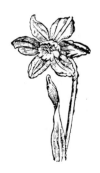

CHAPTER IX.

POSING AND THE MANAGEMENT OF THE SITTER.
THREE-QUARTER LENGTH—LADIES.

HITHERTO I have spoken of the sitter generically as "he," meaning, however, to include both sexes, just as women and children are included in all mankind; but as I am writing this chapter exclusively on ladies, I must alter the sitter's designation for the time being to "she." There is also the apparent absurdity, in writing on this subject, of calling all your models "sitters," although they may not want seated portraits of themselves; but the term is so generally accepted and understood to include all those who go to be represented either by the painter or photographer, that I shall continue to use it.

The female costume, when it suits those who order fashion to have it picturesque, offers greater facilities to the artist who desires variety in his poses than ugly masculine garments will admit of. Besides which, other reasons conduce to the making of more effective pictures when a lady is the subject. A greater range of expression is allowable, and the occupations and amusements of ladies afford many motives and much help to the photographer, while the occasional beauty of the subject encourages the operator by compelling him to make really fine pictures in spite of himself. There is a natural grace about some women and children that gives harmony to their slightest movements, and a fitness to their most trivial acts, so that if they only move across the room, the eye follows them with a similar kind of pleasure to which the ear listens to melodious sounds.

But it is not how to make "beauty go beautifully" that the photographer wants to know, so much as how to manage and make the best of the ordinary sitter who comes to the studio in the course of every-day practice.

Much will depend on the age of the subject, but we will take it for the present that she is neither very old nor very young, neither a young girl nor an elderly matron. Something also must be allowed for the temperament of the sitter; difficult poses should never be tried with nervous or awkward people.

A general rule might be given in very few words: Make your pose very simple, but avoid the "front elevation" or "profile section" effect, to do which you must get variety in the lines of the figure; but in doing so, avoid the twists and contortions so much affected by some photographers. Try to get the feeling of life and motion.

To accomplish this, it is sometimes necessary to make your subject walk round the studio, and suddenly stop at the point where you wish to photograph her, thus getting the effect of suspended motion which is often seen in statues, and gives such an effect of animation when properly managed. The Apollo Belvidere is a well-known example of the kind of pose I mean. The figure is suddenly arrested in its action to watch the flight of the arrow, and stands for a moment in a pose that gives great variety of graceful lines without exaggeration, and could have been easily photographed. But to come down from the classic to the real, let us try to sketch a figure photographed on this principle. And I may mention here that it would be easy to give a set of poses for imitation, but this would be bad for the student if he did not get at the same time the principles on which the pose is based, and learn the causes which lead up to the pose, as in the present example.

A lady walking past a table slightly stoops to pick up a book or a flower, and, raising herself, turns her head to speak to a friend. This action, if made by an easy and graceful figure, is full of animation, and gives great variety. Sitters almost always place both feet flat on the ground as they stand for a portrait; this often produces stiffness. In the pose just described, if the left foot rests on the toe, as in the act of walking, the grace-

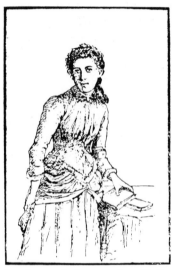

fulness of the action is much increased, and there is more " go " in the figure.

The changes may be rung on this idea for representing figures in suspended motion. A lady sitting at her table or desk rises as a friend enters the room ; she picks up a book, or buttons her glove. These are natural actions, and anything is better than the stiff, self-conscious position so often adopted. In attempting to give life and motion to a figure, avoid going to extremes. There are those who, overstepping the modesty of nature, put too much " gush " into their poses. There are also those of what might be called the invertebrate school, who contort their figures into ridiculously strained attitudes, in their endeavour to make them graceful.

As a rule, for the ordinary lady sitter, there is nothing better than the simple attitude a figure takes when standing in a room with the hands together ; or, for the sake of variety, one hand may be on the table or behind the back, care being taken to avoid any ostentatious display of pose. Let the art conceal the art, and not let the figure suggest the idea that every limb and finger and fold had been adjusted by the operator. On the other hand, it must always be remembered that those portraits which appear the easiest and most natural owe their effect, not to letting nature alone, but to the skill of the photographer in seeing at once what wants correcting, and making the alteration on the instant, before the sitter has had time to tire. The best poser is he who sees at once what he wants, and knows the readiest means of getting it. Some posers are so skilful and full of resource that they take the portrait almost without troubling the sitter, making the sitting, as it were, merely a little episode in the midst of a pleasant conversation. These are the masters of the art, and I am afraid their number is small. The majority of photographers have to painfully feel their way, and (the most conscientious of them, who feel they must not only earn their money, but let their customers see that they are earning it) fidget their sitter about with so many alterations and adjustments, that the resulting picture often represents a much wearied sample of humanity, with all expression of life or feeling worried out of it.

Many photographers cannot get on without the eternal chair, by which they place every standing figure. It is the abuse rather than the use of the chair that is so objectionable. The heavy carved oak chair and *prie-dieu* have been already laughed out of photography, but there is nothing to be said against a neatly-designed drawing-room chair; this piece of furniture is always useful when used judiciously. It is better when its

F

lines are cut up or carried off by other furniture, such as a table behind it; or its too formal lines may be broken by throwing a shawl partly over the back. A black lace shawl is of infinite use in a studio.

Seated figures are usually more easily managed than standing ones, although Chrysos says, in *Pygmalion and Galatea :—*

> "The nature of the seated attitude
> Does not give scope for much variety."

There seems to be so much more for a seated lady to do than when in the standing positions. Reading, working, sewing, drawing, writing, a cup of tea, all lend their aid. A great deal also can be done with a fan, which lends itself admirably to a variety of changes of pose.

It frequently happens that, when all other devices fail, a passable portrait can be got by making the sitter look down, as in reading a book, arranging flowers, knitting or sewing, thus evading the difficulties of staring eyes and open mouths.

The mention of the looking-down pose somehow reminds me that a few words may be profitably said on the hands. One of the most difficult things on the stage, I have heard an old actor say, is what to do with the hands. This is a difficulty that occurs with fuller force to the photographer. Of great pictorial importance when properly employed, they oftener are the cause of a portrait being rejected than any other part of the picture. The one great fault that ladies find is that their hands are too large, even when it can be demonstrated that they are in proportion with the head ; and they will be found to be always so if they have not been taken with a lens of too short a focus, and if they are as sharply defined as the head. This erroneous notion touching the exaggerated size is traditionary.

Before the introduction of photography, which corrected many artistic mistakes, artists used to draw the hands so absurdly small that when the truth was seen in photographs it was not believed. Still, there is some truth in the hands being too large in many photographs, and the fact that to prevent this the hands must be in the same plane as the face, cramps the operator very much in his posing. There are positions of the hand in which it looks much larger than in others, especially where the broad back of it is seen, or where the two hands are joined together in a broad light, and look, at a little distance, like one hand. When the fingers are interlaced the effect is similar, so also when a long wrist is shown without being broken by a bracelet or other means.

It is better, if possible, to let the hand take its own position, and if it does not come gracefully, to try again. To alter the fingers much is seldom very successful, and if the sitter begins to think about her hand, it never looks either graceful or natural. Care should be taken that the light does not fall too flatly or strongly on the hands, so as to increase their apparent breadth or size.

A well-formed hand is a beautiful object, and of great use pictorially. So much was thought of it by the painters of the

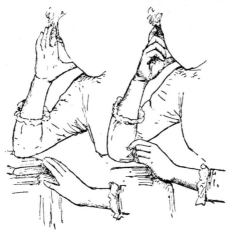

last century, and affectation in posing and displaying the hands was carried to such a pitch, that in some pictures they are the

principal objects, and the heads are accessory. Of course the
great aim in composing a portrait should be to make the head
the principal object, and the hands take the second place.   Care
should be taken that the fingers curve gracefully, and that the
hand does not look like a claw.   That a very little difference
in position will make a vast difference in effect is shown in
the sketches, from photographs of the same hand, on the pre-
ceding page.

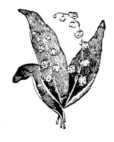

CHAPTER X.

POSING AND THE MANAGEMENT OF THE SITTER. FULL-LENGTH FIGURES.

The full-length figure as a portrait has " gone out." When the carte-de-visite was introduced it assumed this well-known form, and a year or two elapsed before there was any change ; then the head-vignette came in. Photographers stuck to these two forms, and resisted all attempts to add to them for a considerable time. Then the three-quarter figure was introduced, until we came to that monstrosity, the large head that nearly fills the whole space. This last form of card owed its origin to accident. A firm of photographers who possessed a very large stock of negatives of famous people—three-quarter figure, whole-plate size—finding that the carte had quite spoilt the sale of their 8 by 6 portraits, conceived the idea of printing the heads and issuing them as cartes. The ignorant multitude, seeing that so many celebrated characters had had their portraits taken in this way, rushed to have their own done in the same style ; and thus it is that even to this day we are sometimes obliged to do these monstrously out of proportion cards. Some of the earliest full-length cartes-de-visite were pictorial gems. They were done by masters of posing and picture-making. The art had not gone into the hands of the trade then ; prices had not fallen below the usual guinea ; and photographers could afford to give a picture

instead of a map. Cartes of that time by Disderi or Silvy are
still beautiful in pose and effect. Then the art as an art fell upon
evil times. It struck a photograph maker that "ten for ten
shillings" would be a good cry to go to the public with; and
it succeeded, commercially, for sitters followed like flocks of
sheep. They were collected, after paying their money, in a room ;
a door was opened about every five minutes, and a sitter ordered
through it into the studio, where he was fixed up against the
head-rest (always ready), exposed, and shown through another
door, and left to find his way down stairs. There was no
thought given to variety of pose or light and shade ; the only
consideration was how to get the sitters through the studio fast
enough. No proofs were submitted; the sitter had to be content with whatever the manufacturer chose to send him. In
those days people were almost compelled against their will to
carry their cartes in their pocket for the purposes of exchange,
and many did not care for the quality of the portraits, so they
could observe the "social custom" cheaper. This was scarcely
fair to those who went to the best photographers and paid a good
price ; and people objected to exchange the beautiful little
pictures by T. R. Williams, costing, perhaps, seven and sixpence
each, for shilling failures manufactured by a company.

But this is not a history, and I must return from this
digression.

The full-length figure, then, is not so much in vogue as it was
twenty-five years ago. It was never a favourite of mine for
men's portraits, for I cannot be induced to take any interest in
boots and trousers; but it was useful for ladies' portraits,
especially when dresses were worn long; they were not so
easily managed during the short-skirted period, and I am not
sure that it was not the kind of dress that checked the full-length
portraits. The declension of crinoline also was another check, for
it was found difficult to fill up the cabinet form of picture with
the thin figures that succeeded the monstrous balloon figures of a

quarter of a century ago. The full length is still useful, and will, I think, become more prevalent. It still affords the best way of showing gorgeous dresses, fancy costumes, and some portraits, such as those of girls between the age of nine and fifteen. There is a great difficulty in showing the age between these periods. A girl of thirteen or fourteen will often look much older in her portrait if some way is not taken to show that she is a young girl, such as showing that she is wearing a short frock ; and here it is that the full-length is appropriate.

A full-length admits of a more florid treatment than any other style of picture. A more elaborate make-up of the furniture and surroundings is permissible, and pictorial backgrounds may be employed. For ladies' portraits it admits of a greater variety of pose and effect, but it is not so easy to make a pleasing picture of the whole length of a gentleman ; there does not appear to be enough of him to fill the picture ; he is too long for his breadth, and he almost always looks stuck up to be shot at. Let us finish off the gentleman first, as he presents the greatest difficulty. The problem is, how to produce a full-length portrait of a man so that he shall look like a gentleman at his ease, without a preposterous look of attempted dignity, self-consciousness, or defiant swagger on the one hand, or feeble inanity on the other. This is often attempted, but seldom comes off. It is impossible to give rules and regulations in this case, and all that is left for me to do is to tell you what to avoid. If for a standing figure, get some idea of the posture you think would suit the case in hand, and arrange the furniture so that it should lead, as it were, to the pose you require. Then get the model to stand in the place you have prepared for him, and instantly take advantage of all accidents. He may not go into the pose you had in your mind, but if he is not thinking intently on doing his best—which exercise of the faculties spoils half the portraits taken—he will perhaps assume a better. This you must seize at once. It will probably require some slight alteration, some slight turn of the head, or variation in the position of the arm. These are easily made, and can often be done without the model knowing much about it. For example, if you want him to raise his arm, with his hand on his hip, if you will assume this position yourself, you will find in most cases he will with unconscious imitation follow your lead. This will not occur to a blundering operator, one who does not seem to know his own mind; but the skilled operator appears to have a kind of magnetic influence on his sitter which is both curious and useful.

All I have said in the chapter on three-quarter lengths as to variety, movement, animation, &c., applies here, and need not be repeated; but in a full-length there is more scope for what may be called technical art than in any other form of portrait. There is room for the photographer to show his knowledge of composition, a subject into which I have entered fully in " Pictorial Effect " and " Picture-Making by Photography." The student has, I hope, read these little essays, and will know how to arrange his accessories so as to get balance, variety, and contrast.

To make good full-length portraits of ladies is a comparatively easy matter. They are nearly always picturesque in themselves, and, except when an insanity of ugliness seizes those who command the fashions, as it did when the order for wearing crinolettes was issued, their dress lends itself to the needs of the artist. Here again I have said, in a former chapter, everything that is necessary regarding the arrangement of the figure, for what applies to the three-quarter will apply nearly to the full-length; but I may add, what I think has been omitted before, that a lady should never be seated in a very low chair; however easy and natural it may look in life, it often results in the representation of a mere bundle of clothes in a photograph; and if a lady is seated in a high-backed chair it is well to avoid letting the back of the chair rise above each shoulder, which often produces the appearance of deformity.

It is difficult to say anything definite about the posing of ladies without taking the style of dress into consideration. We have passed through a period of seven years distinguished as being the most picturesque and beautiful in regard to ladies' dress that the world has seen for centuries. Æstheticism, however it might be sneered at by the unthinking, or brought into contempt by its too enthusiastic votaries, did wonders for what is known as taste. The reaction that has come has been fortunately only partially successful. The tyrants who rule over fashion, for trade purposes, have perhaps for the first time in the world's history been partly defeated. They ordered that beauty shall be abolished for a season, and ugliness reign. The preposterous forms in which some women now appear is absurd. The curious thing is that they don't see it themselves, and laugh in each other's faces; but they don't even smile at one another. I have just photographed a short lady who, by the curious arrangement of her dress, looked so like a bantam that I almost expected her to crow!

But the reign of ugliness is only partly successful. There was a great revolt against the revolution never before known in the history of fashion. Women are now not the absolute slaves to the dictates of fashion that they have hitherto shown themselves to be throughout the ages. Some of them have been educated, and have learned that taste does not consist entirely in dressing to order to suit trade purposes. Therefore, the most sensible, chiefly the wives and daughters of artists, combined together and signed the pledge against crinolettes! We owe it to this that there are still women to be seen who do not look ridiculous, and who can afford to stand for full-length portraits. In the old crinoline times a lady used to justify herself for her inflated appearance with the pretence, " I must not be singular." That excuse no longer holds. So many sensible women still cling to the good taste they have learnt during the interregnum of crinoline, that there is no pretext for wearing it except absence of taste or a determination to blindly follow the dictates of fashion at all costs.

CHAPTER XI.

POSING AND THE MANAGEMENT OF THE SITTER. GROUPS.

THE arrangement of a portrait group of figures is one of the most difficult things to succeed in accomplishing perfectly in photography; more difficult, certainly, than the composition of a picture that would take a much higher rank in art, but of which the materials were more under the command of the artist as regards selection and disposition. The portrait group is often nothing better than a pile of humanity fitted together like a dissected puzzle; a heterogeneous conglomeration of human atoms, and sometimes dogs, not one of which has any artistic relation to another; agreeing in nothing except that each individual of it shall keep rigid and stare at the lens. The painters also have felt the difficulty of making such an arrangement of a group that the results should be a picture without any sacrifice of the portraits. These things are managed better now than they were before the introduction of photography. Everyone is familiar with the ordinary family picture of orange-holding or mythological women and children immortalised by Goldsmith; or, as Byron describes a family group—

> "A lady with her daughters or her nieces,
> Shine like a guinea and seven-shilling pieces."

The photographer is nearly always heavily handicapped by

having to give an equally good portrait of each individual in the group, while one of the great principles of art is that one component of a picture shall be more prominent and conspicuous than another. In a pictorial group a back is often useful as a contrast to the other figures; but this is not permissible in such groups as are usually demanded from the photographer. Every face must present a favourable portrait, independent of the others; no figure must be sacrificed for the sake of pictorial effect, and therefore there can be little contrast or subordination, so necessary in artistic arrangement. This difficulty is felt by painters who can devote time and attention to each figure, and who also have the great advantage of being able to place their figures on different planes. This absolute necessity for placing all the figures in one plane, so that they may all be in focus, is not so stringent as it was before the introduction of gelatine plates. We can now employ lenses that cover a greater depth of focus than the old portrait lenses, and this enables us to get greater separation in the figures.

The group is the one thing that the photographer dreads, especially if there is to be a baby or young child in it, for as the weakest link is the strength of the chain, so everything depends upon the quietude of a part that can only be depended on to move. However well the photographer may have arranged the other figures, and however strong may have been his injunctions to them as to how they should stand, and in which direction they should turn their faces during the exposure, they have to be vigilantly looked after, and this is almost impossible while you have to devote all your attention to keeping quiet a restless child. Moreover, the baby is always expected to be made a conspicuous point in the picture, and it is so comparatively small an object that it forms nothing more than a minute speck in the group. It is my experience that few people have any idea how small a baby is until they see it in the centre of a group of grown-up persons.

Groups are taken both in the studio and out of doors. We will begin with the former.

Rejlander used to say that it tasks the skill and attention of the photographer quite enough to see that the arrangement, lighting, and expression of one figure is perfect, and he never ventured upon more, if he could help it, except in combination pictures. But portrait photographers cannot always select their subjects, and must make the best of the material brought to them. Now, the most frequent group upon which the photographer is called to operate is that which is composed of two persons, often children—I hope to give the latter a chapter to themselves—but often of grown-up people, and perhaps most frequently, in holiday towns, young people on their honeymoon, who always seem to be animated with the very praiseworthy desire to have their portraits taken in their new relation. This is one of the easiest groups to take if managed well, but one of the most difficult if it is trifled with. As a rule, the best composition can be got if the lady is in a standing position, and the gentleman sitting. It need not be in a chair or in any very formal attitude, but on a table, or the end of a balustrade. This latter accessory, like all imitations, may be very good or very bad; it should not look clean-cut and new, and care should be taken not to make it prominent. If the picture under consideration is to be a three-quarter length—the most convenient form, perhaps—very little of the balustrade will show. Suppose, then, the gentleman sitting on, and the lady standing beside it. They need not be looking at each other; it is not often that a young couple can do this under the circumstances without laughing, but a common source of interest should be found or imagined. It is easy to suppose they were talking to a friend who does not appear in the picture, or that their attention is called to some interesting object. Resort should be had to any device to give the effect of life and movement to the group, and animation to the heads, and to take away

that uneasy and penitential look of being sorry for it, so often
seen in pictures of the kind.   Here are a couple of sketches of
variations on this theme, which may serve as hints for arrangement.

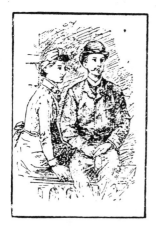 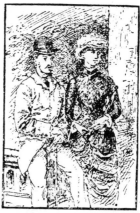

Where the balcony is used, or any other outdoor accessory, it
is well to use also an outdoor background.

Very agreeable pictures may be made with two young ladies
for the subject.   In this case there are plenty of motives for the
picture.   The occupations of ladies seem to lend themselves to
pictorial effect.

It is perhaps easier to make a well-composed group of three
figures than of two.   With two it is sometimes difficult to get
variety of line, or a picturesque general form to the group; but
with three figures the opportunities for variety, contrast, and a
pyramidal form to the group, are much greater.   So that the
unity of the group is preserved, the greatest amount of variety
of form should be sought for.   Variety in position of the heads
can easily be got.   It is possible with almost any three figures
to arrange the heads so that they do not come exactly in a line

with each other. For instance, it would be possible to arrange
the heads formally, thus—

O

O O

but it is quite as easy and much more pleasant to break the
uniformity, and arrange them thus—

O

O

O

The same principle is carried out in the group of three
children—

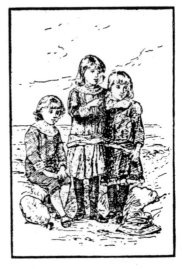

If more than three figures are required in a group, it is better
to turn the camera on its side, and make a horizontal picture of
it. Indeed, in many cases when only three are included, the
horizontal form is very useful, as in the following example.

By placing three children at a table, the difficulties of feet
and legs are got rid of, and the heads can be got larger without

making the children look older than they are, the table and book suggesting scale. When the heads are all nearly of the same

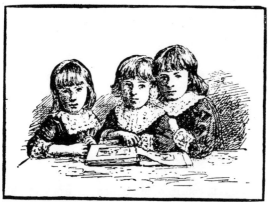

height, variety may be got by placing one of them at a distance from the other two.

In a group of adults, it is well to get some centre of interest, such as reading a letter, as in the last illustration to this

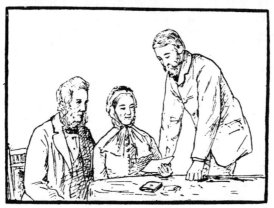

chapter; but care must always be taken not to sacrifice likeness to composition. One of the chief difficulties is to get the heads close together without appearing forced and unnatural.

CHAPTER XII.

POSING AND THE MANAGEMENT OF THE SITTER. OUTDOOR GROUPS.

WHEN a group is to consist of more than three or four individuals, it is often convenient to take it out of doors. There are several advantages in getting out of the studio; you are not cramped for room, and need not pile your sitters together, as you are often compelled to do in the small space available in most studios. The exposure will be much quicker, taking not more than one or two seconds with a rapid rectilinear lens, and smaller diaphragms may be used than would be possible in the studio; the greater depth of focus thus gained allowing much wider freedom in the artistic arrangement of the group.

An outdoor group too often represents a mass of figures placed one over the other on a bank, with perhaps a brick wall for a background, without any attempt at artistic arrangement, like the sketch, which is copied from a photograph, or a row of figures set up to be photographed, without any consideration as to their arrangement, except to get them in focus. This latter disposition is sometimes caused by the impossibility of getting any help from the formation of the ground or place where the photograph has to be taken, for it nearly always happens that the large groups are taken "at home," and the photographer must do the best with the materials he can find. He should look out for and take advantage of any spot that would aid him in breaking up his group, and giving variety to the general forms ; if he should find a picturesque set of steps, he may consider himself fortunate ; even one or two steps are better than nothing. In selecting his background, he should endeavour to secure one with a broad expanse of light, such as a light wall, if not too blank. Much detail is objectionable, as it interferes with the figures. The worst background, but the one that is

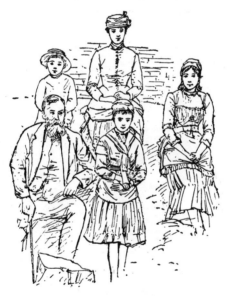

oftenest used for groups, consists of foliage, especially when laurel or any shrubs with large shining leaves have place. The effect of the white spots produced by the glittering foliage, especially when out of focus, is very disagreeable.

I give an illustration in which a flight of steps leading up to the door of an old Gothic house has greatly aided the photographer in arranging a portrait group.

When you have to arrange a group, you should begin by

finding out the most important persons in the company, so that
you may assign them conspicuous places.   In a short time you
will be able to discover "the funny man."   There is always one
in every group, who thinks it a rare joke to make some of the
others laugh and spoil the negative.   More groups are damaged
by this idiot than by any other cause.   Everything must give
way to his wit, and it takes a spacious magnanimity to endure
his buffoonery.   You must neutralise him, or you will do no

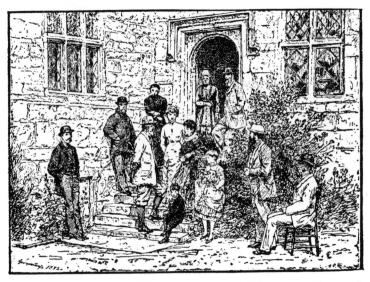

good.   If you have courage enough, go boldly up to him, and
say something to this effect :—" So you are the funny man, are
you?   If I can get on with you, I can easily manage all the rest.
If you will kindly suppress yourself for a few minutes, and let
me have my turn, I shall be much obliged."   He takes this
usually in one of two ways—either he is a good fellow who sees
a brother-joker in you, and does all he can to help you ; or he
sulks.   Either way will suit your purpose.   In the illustration
you will easily recognise the suppressed funny man in the one

set against the wall, where he makes a capital balance to the principal group, and looks, in the original photograph, as if he had not quite made up his mind whether he ought to be ashamed of himself or not.

By this time you have got to some knowledge of the different members of the group, and have settled in your mind, approximately, how they are to be arranged. When you have quite made up your mind, and not till then, and when the camera is quite ready, place your figures. Don't make experiments or changes if you can help it; in other words, don't look like a muff, but let the members of the group see that you know what you are about, and mean to carry out the arrangement that you have mentally formed.

I have seen operators make an ostentatious display of the trouble they were taking, as if they were expected to earn their money by the sweat of their brow, making numerous changes until they wearied out their victims. People are quite up to this sort of display now, and laugh at it—until it becomes too serious.

In a well-designed group the principal rules of art will be observed, especially variety, balance, contrast, and breadth. Every line and form will be so arranged that a series of pyramids, intersecting and mingled with each other, are created. In the illustration, those to whom it was thought advisable to give most prominence are in the centre, and form a pyramidal group to themselves, but they become part of a series of pyramids, all blended into one, of which the top of the arch of the door is the apex. It may also be noticed of what extreme value a bit of pure black or white becomes when in the right place. In the photograph—it is not so easy to show it in the small cut —the white hat of the standing figure to the right absolutely redeems the group from failure. Imagine it away, and there is no artistic solidity in the group. This one small spot of white in the right place keeps everything together.

In the second group the place was different, and there was not so good an opportunity of forming a fine group. The ground was flat, and there was no natural means of raising any of the figures above the others; the photographer had therefore to be content to break the line by seating some of his figures, and making others bend as though talking to them. By this means he succeeded in forming a series of varied pyramidal forms running into and connected with each other, so that the general effect should not be scattered. There should always be a " oneness "

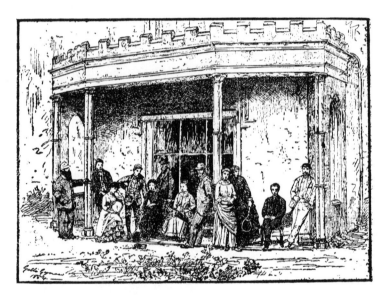

in the group; the string should run through all the beads, but should be more felt than seen.

There is another vast difference between the two groups; the first has for its surroundings a corner of a very fine Tudor Hall, partly overgrown with old English shrubs; the second is a sham Gothic battlemented verandah, protecting a large French window —an incongruous mixture—and the foreground consists of the geraniums, calceolarias, violas, and other kindred plants of an Italian garden.

There are some disadvantages about taking groups, and portraits generally, out of doors, the chief of which is the difficulty with the expressions from the excess of light. Some people are more affected by this than others; these should be carefully looked after, and so arranged that the light should be of the least annoyance to them. A portrait group should never be taken in sunlight if there is any possibility of avoiding it.

It sometimes happens that you have to get some other hand to expose. If you have to depend on a quite inexperienced person, it is as well to explain to him that the cap must be removed from *before* the lens as well as off it. I have sometimes seen the cap taken off and held in front of the lens. There is a certain butler who exposes a group in which the writer annually appears, who talks learnedly of seconds and fractions of seconds, and firmly believes that he takes the photographs.

CHAPTER XIII.

POSING AND THE MANAGEMENT OF THE SITTER. CHILDREN.

THERE was a time when children were looked upon with dread by the photographer, and I knew two or three studios where they were absolutely refused. This was in the days when sitters were as plentiful as blackberries in autumn, and professional pleasure in overcoming difficulties was quite subsidiary to the number of guineas taken.

The true photographer will always take delight in a difficult sitter, just as a surgeon does in a beautiful case of compound fracture, or a physician in some obscure disease. To go on exposing a long succession of plates on easy subjects soon becomes monotonous; it is when a sitter calls for your reserve powers that he becomes interesting. There are certainly some bad sitters who are very depressing, with no redeeming points about them, such as those who begin by saying they hate being taken, following this pleasant observation up with the worn-out joke about it being as bad as going to the dentist. It is a very curious thing how they all bring this ancient pleasantry out as if it was perfectly original, and a fine sample of wit. It is not very exciting amusement to work this sort of customer round into a happy frame of mind; but there is to me something almost fascinating about a fractious three-year-old who objects to have his portrait taken.

In a case of this kind it is your duty to so work upon that child that he shall not only willingly do all you require, but shall be so delighted with you that he shall howl when he is taken away after the operation, and will only be pacified by a promise that he shall come again.

"How is this to be done?" may well be asked. There are two things of primary importance. The child must not be forced, and mothers and nurses must be rigidly suppressed. When I have had a few minutes' interview with a child, I easily discover if it has been worried, and spoilt for my purpose by some bungling photographer who has so frightened it that it dreads to enter a studio; or if it has been —shall I say tampered with?—by the mother or nurse. These latter will think they are doing the right thing when they solemnly impress upon the little sitters that they must be very good and keep quite still; but their well-intentioned warnings produce exactly the reverse effect to what is wanted. The child that insists upon being good is an unmitigated nuisance; he will do everything you ask him to do, and looks as wooden as an awkward lay figure.

With the great majority of children the battle is won or lost at the first introduction. The clever photographer will decide at a glance whether the child belongs to one of these classes— the fearless child who takes the sitting as part of the day's occupation, and enjoys it; the nervous child, who really would be good, but has a constitutional fear of any new experience; and, worst of all, the shy child. The first of these is easily managed; the chief thing to bear in mind is, that the first of him will be the best, and that the sooner you take him the better. As he gets to know you—familiarity breeds contempt —he will become less manageable. He will continue to smile and be very good and agreeable, but you will find that after a few exposures he will quietly slip off the chair, or run away from where you have placed him when you turn to go to the camera. He approves of you, and wants to have a lark with you. But when very young children begin to play practical jokes, I know no cure for the disease except sending them home to meditate on their sins, to come again another day if the exposures you have already made do not produce satisfactory pictures.

The nervous child wants very gentle management. It is no use attempting to proceed at once to serious business in a case of this kind. The subject must be led up to gradually. The photographer had better meet her—it is usually a girl—in the reception room, and quietly introduce himself. This leads to showing and getting her interested in pictures, when the nervousness will probably begin to wear off. In my studio I have an intermediate room between the reception room and the studio proper. The place is full of things interesting to children, and I find it very useful in gradually breaking the nervous little patient in before my horrid purpose is fully divulged. If, after a few minutes' talk and looking at pictures, you should happen to have a squeaking toy or a musical box in your pocket, and you begin a gentle performance on it, you will have nearly got that child into a proper state of mind for a sitting—or, at all events, for going through the needful arrangements in the dressing room. At first the child should not be allowed to see the toy ; it should be an invisible performance—something for the mind of the patient to dwell on and wonder at during the dressing operation. By this time, if you have not mismanaged, you will have so " coralled the sympathies " of the child that she will have lost much of her fear of you; and, if you will allow her nurse to keep close to her, she will permit you to jump her up on a table, and even, if you do not bungle or hurry it, place the head-rest. When nervous children get over the first exposure, and find it does not hurt them, they usually become very good sitters. But there are children whose nervousness it is almost impossible to overcome. These have either suffered from a medical operation, or from the dentist, or, worst of all, they have had a bad quarter of an hour with a bungling or brutal photographer who had no patience or care for the management of children, and had to try to do by force what ought to have been done by guile. Photographers should recognise the fact that their principal weapon with children is "wheedling," although there are, I admit, some cases in which a moderate degree of firmness is useful.

The shy child is extremely difficult to manage. She is not afraid of you, but simply shy, and endeavours to get behind her mother or nurse, and hide herself in her dress. In these cases it is often better not to try much persuasion—except, perhaps, a gentle attempt to make friends—but to proceed to the studio and go on with the sitting at once. A shy child will often take the sitting as a matter of course if it is done quickly, but would become troublesome if allowed time to think.

In all these classes there are, of course, all degrees and varieties, but I can only write generally on the treatment of the class; the photographer must modify his entertainment to suit individual cases; but if he is kind, quiet, patient, and judicious, he will not lose above one or two per cent. of the children brought to him for their portraits.

It is curious to observe the different idiosyncracies of children. The photographer will find it useful to classify them as I have done above; but there are many species in each genus. Notice the different ways they have of objecting to be photographed. Some object right out, and fight and scream against it. This is mere brute force opposition, without any subtlety in it; but some children, you would almost think, had studied resistance as a fine art.

If a child fights, it is of no use to oppose force by force. Nurses will often attempt this, but you must stop them at once. The child must be a willing victim, or it must be sent away to come again another day. When a child will not sit, try to find out the cause. Analyse the subject as you would a problem in mathematics. Probably the mother is in the room; now mothers are a very useful institution, but they are terribly in the way when their children are to be photographed. Turn her out with all the civility you can command. You must then ask the nurse to do everything you direct intelligently and quickly, but on no account to help when not asked, as she may be doing something exactly opposite to what you required. The ground will now be cleared for dealing with your sitter; the time he has had to himself will have probably altered his convictions, and he will submit; if not, shake hands with him, and wish him good-bye, as you only want good children to play with. If this and other blandishments do not fetch him, let him go. The visit has done him no harm, and he will remember things that he would like to see again, and on a second visit will probably sit without any trouble.

It would be tedious to consider separately every variation in the characters of children, but if the photographer would succeed with these delightful little troubles, he must have great patience, a genuine delight in a difficult subject, and a strong determination to succeed with it. Above all, he must establish perfect confidence between himself and his sitter, to do which he must descend to the level of the child, and, remembering that little things please little minds, be able to enter into childish games, tell childish tales, and, above all, to play with toys!

Before concluding this subject, I must say a word or two on expression. The most beautiful thing about the most beautiful child is nearly always its expression. This can only be educed by stratagem, and should demand the greatest efforts of the photographer. A simple pose, such as sitting on a table (which, for a three-quarter vignette, is a very suitable position), will suit a child better than any elaborate arrangement, so that your attention shall not be unduly distracted from the bringing out of the best expression.

You will, of course, have a whole battery of toys ready when required to amuse your little sitters, for toys are the stock-in-trade of childhood, and he who understands their use and mystery best will soonest become at one with his subject. I should strongly recommend you to keep them strictly for your own use. If the child sees they belong to you, and can only be got through you, you will become a much more interesting person to him, and consequently have more power. If you allow the nurse to have the run of the collection, she will show them all at once, or quickly one after the other, and their power for use will be gone. Some toys are more adapted to keep children quiet, or awaken their expression, than others—those to which they have to listen, for instance. The ticking of a watch is the most familiar of these, but it must be a loud-ticking one, or the effort to hear will put too much strain into the expression. A musical box is good, but rather too elaborate; any toy that is new to the child is good, but those that have something comic about them, and make a noise, are best. I have found some of the india-rubber toys that squeak when pressed very effective.

There are some children who will sit as you place them without any trouble; but when you are thinking what an easy job you have got, and put your hand on the cap of the lens, you find them making faces. This generally takes the form of an awe-struck opening of the mouth. This is a case difficult to treat. You will not be so unwise as to tell it to close its lips, for to mention any feature to a child is to make it think of that feature, and proceed to contort it at once. Perhaps if you have not warned her, the injudicious nurse tells it to shut its mouth, and the good, obedient little thing will at once close it so firmly that there is nothing more to be done until the child has forgotten it. I have found that the best way to deal with a case of this kind is simply to touch the child on the lower lip, and the mouth will assume its natural position.

I have made this chapter on posing children already too long without saying anything about posing them, making it something

CHAPTER XIV.

POSING AND THE MANAGEMENT OF THE SITTER. EXPRESSION IN PORTRAITURE.

" EVERY man is as God made him, and oftentimes a great deal worse," said Sancho Panza ; and, if we may judge by the productions of the majority of photographers, his opinion is singularly true. Let us not blind ourselves to the fact that ordinary photographs are very ordinary indeed. The dead level of good work has spread like a disease, and he is a very poor photographer who cannot take a passably good portrait—one that, seen by itself, would pass muster as real gold with the average unobservant person, but which would turn out mere tinsel when placed side by side with the work of a master. It would be difficult to at once tell what was the difference. An old friend of mine used to say that it was "That!" accompanying the word with a snap of the fingers, by which he meant to express that last touch by which genius carries its work just beyond the goal reached by mere talent—a mystery which it is impossible to explain, but which is felt in all art. In photographic portraiture it will be found to depend almost entirely on the expression of the face, aided by the attitude of the figure, which should be in keeping with the expression, and be easy and characteristic. To obtain the best expression, the photographer should be not only an art student, but a student of human nature. He should not only be able to pose his model in a graceful or appropriate position, to place him in an effective light, and to get a good technical negative of him, but, if he is to be the ideal photographer,

"That perfect monster which the world ne'er saw,"

he must be able to sum up his sitter at a first introduction, and determine at once, amongst other things, the expression which would best suit that face, and to work up to that expression during the usually brief interval which elapses between introduction and exposure.

Have you ever noticed, when you are about to take a portrait, and are endeavouring to call up an animated expression on the countenance of your sitter, what a dogged determination he sometimes has, not to be beguiled out of the moody expression he has assumed? At last, when you have tried all the subtleties you know, you ask him, in desperation, if he has not got such a trifle as a smile with him. He immediately answers, with a charming expression you long to secure, "Oh, no! when I smile in a photograph I always grin." Here is another sample of a good model gone wrong through the stupidity of photographers. Many operators think that if they make their sitters smile— they don't care about the quality of the smile—they have done their duty in their own particular state of life, forgetting that many people look idiotic when their simpers and smiles are perpetuated. Others seem to think that all expression consists of gush, and wake up the features to an unnatural degree of intensity. The photographer should endeavour to represent his sitters as moderately calm ladies and gentlemen; or, if they are not entitled to the courtesy title, then as decent men and women.

Some faces are beautiful in repose, hideous in movement. A broad laugh is often beautiful in nature, because of its evanescence; it becomes intolerable when fixed on paper. But there is a look of animation, far short of a smile, which suits nearly all faces, and which is so permanently beautiful that it deserves to be printed in carbon or enamel.

John Gibson, the famous sculptor, considered a smile frivolous; but what would be undignified in sculpture may be proper to less severe modes of artistic expression. He says, in a letter to a friend :—"The fault of the portraits of the present age is, that every man is expected to look pleasant in his pictures. The old masters represent men thinking, and women tranquil; the Greeks the same. Therefore, the past race of portraits in paint and in marble look more like a superior class of beings. How often have I heard the remark, ' Oh! he looks too serious.' But the expression that is meant to be permanent should be serious and calm."

This is true enough of the expressions of men, but I cannot help feeling that the cheerful expressions of ladies and children are their best, especially when they are educed with such art as to appear perfectly natural; indeed, some of the most delightful portraits of children represent them in a very happy frame of mind.

The quality necessary in a man to enable him to draw out the best expression is " a gift." It may be improved by education and practice, but it is not to be attained by those who have it not in their natures. The latter may do high-class work, but never that which electrifies. A fine work should always give that feeling of pleased surprise which sends a glow of pleasure through the frame. This is never obtained through the intervention of that photographer who has not the proper "music in his soul."

When a man goes to have his portrait taken, his mind will, consciously or unconsciously, dwell upon the ordeal he is to go through; he will think of how his coat fits, how he feels, and how he will look; it should be the business of the photographer to make him forget all this—and himself. The man's appearance is positively deteriorated by constant reference to self, and the consideration of how he looks when sitting for a portrait. Now what that phase conveys is exactly that which should be avoided. It is needless to tell photographers that one-half their sitters think they know how to sit, and it is equally unnecessary to add that this knowing moiety are his worst subjects.

The kind of conversational treatment that would best suit every sitter must be left for each photographer to decide for himself.

Everything so much depends on small things that it would be difficult to say much about them without opening a wider subject than is here intended; but the photographer would find that it would simplify his labour, and be a kind of aid to thought, if he made a rough classification of his sitters, such as those who are best left alone. These are those who are ordered to have their portraits taken by their friends, and do not care how it is done; they usually obey the photographer's directions without question, and their portraits are always natural. The nervous, who require very delicate treatment; those whom a bluff treatment would suit, and those who claim the greatest show of respect; and, above all, those who "hate being photographed." These last-mentioned are the sort I like if I have time to deal with them properly. It makes one feel a professional pride to so work these difficult sitters that they shall feel that although they came to you with reluctance, they leave with regret. This, I find, is often the case with children. They will sometimes scream at being brought, and scream at being taken away. Then there is that much respected person who thinks he can teach you your business—the best way is to listen and learn. No man can speak without saying something.

A great deal of expression, and that of the most agreeable kind, may be produced by the action of the figure, as well as by the feature. Appropriate action may give life and animation to a subject not otherwise attainable. A man would not look very happy if he held down his head, and tucked in his chin, smiled he never so pleasantly; while a very little animation in the features will have an agreeable effect if it is properly backed up and assisted by an animated turn of the head; but, at the same time, straining after expression must be avoided; the happy mean is what the judicious photographer should strive for and get.

Some photographers seem to do all they know to awe their sitters into their worst expressions. A lady who was recently sitting to me told me her experiences in getting her portrait taken in a well-known studio in London. An appointment was made beforehand. The door was opened by a man-servant in a gaudy livery. The lady was ushered upstairs, and kept waiting for half-an-hour, with nothing to amuse her but the solemn grandeur of the place. In the studio there were three photographers to attend to her; one to work the camera, another to move the furniture and place the head-rest, and a third in white kid gloves to take command of the posing. The two latter talked over the personal appearance of the sitter as if she was an unintelligent lay figure, which she says she felt she had become before the exposure commenced, and she looks like it in the print.

I cannot understand how it is possible to make the sitter feel at his ease if the operator has a lot of assistants to help him. Sitting for a portrait should be a matter for friendly intimacy between sitter and photographer, not a solemn ceremony.

Those who still look at photography with withering contempt —and some such exist to the present day, just as it is thought that rare individuals of the plesiosaurus are yet to be found in the deep seas—complain that photography has no power to idealise; but if they had any knowledge of our mysteries, they would know that it is no longer the truthful art it was when it was famous for having no mercy.

These critics take it as a foregone conclusion that a portrait should be idealised. The notion that the artist should invest

H

his sitters with a grace not their own seems never to have been doubted. Dr. Johnson said that it was one of the highest proofs of the genius of Reynolds that he contrived to give nobleness to the head of Goldsmith in his portrait, whose genial soul and fine intellect were not habited in a very dignified or handsome body. If Reynolds gave to Goldsmith a nobility of countenance which nature had denied, but which the painter conceived was more characteristic of the inner man than the actual present-ment, then we have in the portrait Reynolds' conception of what Goldsmith ought to have looked like, and not the actual portrait of the man. If he merely depicted him at his best, happily catching the expression which lit up the face when it was aglow with some happy thought, then he did not give Goldsmith the noble look, but, with the true painter's skill, readily detected the noblest effect, and gave permanent form to a transient expression; he did what every photographer should try to do, and when he succeeds he may expect to hear the sitter's friends exclaim—

"Masterly done :
The very life seems warm upon the lips ;
The fixture of the eye has motion in it,
And we are mocked by art."

CHAPTER XV.

POSING AND THE MANAGEMENT OF THE SITTER. SUGGESTION AND INTERFERENCE IN POSING.

THE photographer is often annoyed by the ridiculous suggestions made by the friends of the sitter, and sometimes by the sitter himself, although the latter oftener takes the character of a hopeless victim.

It is a question how far such interference is to be tolerated, and how it is to be met.

Many photographers object to their sitters being accompanied by a friend, and prefer to have them to themselves. I do not agree with this exclusion, and always welcome the presence of one or two of the sitter's friends, if they are not fussy people, and gladly accept their hints and suggestions if they are made at the proper time—that is, before I begin to pose the model; any interference after I have begun is sure to do mischief. Everything depends upon the temperament of the sitter. She —it is the ladies generally who object to come alone—may like to have a friend with her to give her confidence, but prefers not to be looked at as the exposure is going on. It is always easy to manage in a case of this sort. The friend may turn away her head, or sit behind a curtain; in my own place I have a sort of ante-room to the studio, made attractive and comfortable, into which I send the friends when I find they are doing mischief by remaining in the studio. This is sufficiently near to satisfy the most nervous sitter, and they do not interfere with the operation. It is the practice of some photographers not to permit anyone to be present, but it is not wise to draw a hard-and-fast line. It should be absolutely at the sitter's choice whether friends should be present or not; it is surely better to humour the sitter and get a good portrait, than to have your own way entirely and an inferior production. When the friends have left the studio they should remain away until the exposure has taken place. Nothing is more disturbing than people going in and out. Above all, never allow peeping. Friends will sometimes go away, and then creep quietly back and peep through the door or through a curtain. Nothing could be more calculated to make the sitter nervous than this sort of thing, and it quite prevents all endeavours to try what might be called experimental expression. Sitters are often inclined to think they lose dignity if they do not look dignified. It is often possible to talk them into a genial state, or get them to act the part—" assume a virtue if they have it not "—but this is quite out of the question if you or the sitter feels all the time that there is some one taking a surreptitious peep, and listening to all that is said.

Having made it clear that I do not object to two or three of the friends of the sitter being present, let us see how far these visitors may be allowed to interfere.

Information is always valuable, and any information a photographer can get he should be thankful for, and use at his discretion. Of course, the size and style of the picture required has been settled in the reception room; but it is often of great advantage to get some further knowledge than can be obtained at first sight of your subject. It is well to know if former photographers have failed, and why. Was it expression, pose, dress, bad photography, or what? Useful hints of what to avoid can easily be gathered, and you may learn what is best to be done by judicious conversation ; you should also find out the sort of thing that would be likely to please, such as any characteristic attitude or expression. All this will aid you in getting a picture that the friends will declare is " *so* like." I need not say that you should find out whether a sitting or standing pose would be preferred. It often happens that after the operator has taken the number of negatives he thinks necessary or desirable to use in the particular case, and the job is, in fact, finished, some kind friend will suggest that she should so like to have " one in a hat." This you would have been very glad to do if you had known in time, but it is difficult to refuse, and you expose another plate. This might have been avoided if proper enquiries had been made at the outset.

Then there are those who want to see the pose, and will promise to go away when you are ready. These people are not easy to deal with. It is difficult to explain to them before the sitter that you may possibly want to surprise her into a characteristic attitude or expression ; that would be to expose your carefully masked plot, and moreover, if you do let them stay, they will, perhaps, not go at the last minute, and the sitter will feel constrained, and tire while you are getting them out. My rule is, in *or* out, just as the sitter pleases, but not in *and* out on any pretext.

There are some people who are quite irrepressible. They promise not to interfere, and mean to keep their promise, but for all that jump up just as the cap is about to be removed from the lens to alter a bit of drapery or set a lock of hair straight, or to make a brilliant suggestion, such as that the pose of the hands might be improved—when you are taking the head only ! They knew very well that the hands would not be in the picture, but such people cannot restrain themselves, and should be got rid of if possible. When these vexing little incidents occur, it is better to break off, make the sitter walk round the room, and begin again.

Some sitters will bring a friend to pose them. "It is such an advantage, you know, to have the assistance of an artist," they will perhaps insult you by saying, on the strength of their friend having passed the second grade examination in free-hand, or copied some smudgy flowers on terra cotta, but who, nevertheless, has never heard of composition. Of all the irritating assistance the photographer has offered to him, that of the amateur artist is the most difficult to accept smiling—or, perhaps, I should say, *without* smiling. The highly trained artist is bad enough, as I shall presently show; but the combined ignorance and assurance of the amateur is quite fatal.

Then there are those who kindly endeavour to teach you your business—who explain that hands come large if placed too forward; that blue photographs badly, that yellow does not "take," and that photographs taken abroad are better than those done in this country, because the light is clearer; and, finally, those who prefer to give you their instructions in learned words suited to the occasion, just as they would talk to a foreigner in his own tongue—and puzzle him. These wise ones want their portrait to be " a small focus," or " a large focus," and are surprised if you tell them that there are no different sizes of focus, and that focus has no other dimension than length.

How much help you are to admit in dealing with young folks, I have alluded to incidentally in the chapter on photographing children. It is quite impossible to get on if children are accompanied by a troop of friends, especially lively grandfathers and grandmothers. A father may sometimes be admitted if he be of an exceptional sort, but even in his case it is better to keep him in reserve for use if the usual means fail. Nine out of ten mothers are useful, but the tenth should be kept out of the studio. A nurse who knows her business is the best help you can have. Even she will sometimes want a standing portrait of a ten-month old baby, but it is easier to tell the nurse she is an idiot than the mother.

It might be thought that artists, and those who have been trained to art, would be able to give very efficient advice in the studio; but I have found it quite to the contrary, and this invariably. Even experienced portrait painters are very much at a loss how to pose a sitter for the photographer, although they may require the photograph for their own use, and may have had time to consider the matter. The fact is, that painters are in the habit of going about their work in a more leisurely manner than photographers, and cannot pose quickly. They find it to their advantage to go quietly to work, as they can call up expression when they want it, or leave it to a future sitting; while the photographer knows that if he harasses his sitter too much, he knocks the life out of him. Yet there are some photographers who gladly accept the aid of a brother artist if he can prove that he really is skilful in his business.

There is a story that once upon a time, when an illustrious prince and his noble entertainer returned from deer-stalking, they sent for a photographer to make a pictorial record of their successful day's sport. When the stags were being arranged, Sir Edwin Landseer, who was present, made some suggestions for the improvement of the composition of the group. The photographer resented this interference, declaring that he could not get on if those who knew nothing about art altered his arrangements. "But I am Sir Edwin Landseer," said the great artist; "surely you know my pictures." "Oh! if you are in the trade it is all right," replied the photographer, and gladly accepted Sir Edwin's assistance.

To conclude. Be strong, but hide your strength; be gentle in manner, but vigorous in the deed; make up your mind what you mean to do, and do it. If your sitter or her friends think all the credit is due to themselves, let them think so. It pleases them, and does not hurt you; in fact, it is in your favour, for they will like the picture all the better if they fancy its merits are due to their own valuable suggestions.

CHAPTER XVI.

SMILES AND SMILING.

A REALLY beautiful smile, natural, and without the taint of artifice, is one of the rarest, as well as the most delightful, inventions of nature. The tendency in the zygomatic muscles to contract under pleasurable emotions, to speak scientifically, is a joy reserved for mankind alone, for the hyæna does not laugh, whatever unscientific natural historians may say to the contrary. Not that I should like to assert too positively that all animals have not some equivalent method for displaying their emotions, for surely many of them show rudimentary attempts at expression in their faces.

Some dogs, for instance, can convey an easily-interpreted expression of their feelings by their looks. The other morning I asked a friendly terrier, belonging to a neighbour, to go for a walk. There was a most distinct look of pleasure on that dog's face as he frisked around when he accepted the invitation, and I fancied I could detect an upward curl of the mouth; there was certainly a twinkle in the eye. It happened that after I had walked a mile from home, I went into a shop, leaving the dog to wait outside. I stayed longer than I intended, and left by a different door to the one by which I entered, forgetting my canine friend. Since that time I have never been able to induce that dog to take any notice of me, except to put on a dejected, disgusted visage whenever I approach. His feelings were hurt, and he did not care to conceal it.

That rudimentary expressions are to be traced in animals, goes to prove that the smile, like man himself, is the result of evolution, and that the perfected smile is the product of civilisation. We do not know how far this can be traced back; all we do know is that an oyster can be crossed in love, but we cannot definitely ascertain that he is capable of smiling at grief, like patience on a monument.

The smile, then, being a product of civilisation, is capable of being overdone, and of becoming unnatural, as, indeed, is the tendency of all cultivated things; and it is this false smile that gives the conscientious photographer more trouble than any other phase of expression. The unconscious smile, that perfect expression of happiness, seems to be dying out. It is rarely present even in children, especially when they are in the hands of the photographer, however sympathetic he may be. Who amongst us does not constantly observe that painful nervous contraction of the lips and elongation of mouth seen in many children when they are being photographed? Parents and nurses are a good deal to blame for this. They impress on the young people, before they take them to the studio, that they must be still, and, above all, must look pleasant. Now what is the effect on its appearance of telling a child to be good? If it is of a kindly disposition, it will become prim; if the demon that seems to possess some children's souls has possession of it, it will become sullen. Then, being dressed specially for the occasion has its effect. It is impossible for a child used to the enjoyment, in easy-fitting clothes, of the rollicking pleasures of the nursery, to appear at its ease in its "Sunday best," yet its natural guardians not only overdress the child, but will sometimes go even further, and try on unaccustomed garments and new ways of doing the hair. Now to dress a child in stiff clothes, different from its ordinary wear, to alter the style of hair, and to solemnly impress upon the poor little mite that it must be good and smile, is to kill that child as a subject for the photographer. It is sometimes possible for a clever operator to make a modern young person forget all the world, and become "even as a little child" again, but the exertion is more than some photographers are equal to. So the natural smile is dying out, killed through the folly of mothers and nurses when they prepare their children for being photographed. I am glad we have been able to trace this growing defect of nature to its origin!

Mothers and nurses know so little of children! They are incredulous when told that infants never smile, but that it comes to them as they grow. The art of smiling has to be learnt by experience, and, perhaps, at that early age, infants have no happy thoughts to smile at—have not attained the power to see "those undiscerned phantasms that make a chrisom child to smile." Mr. Darwin, who seems to have gathered up all facts in nature, describes his observations on this point in a characteristic passage:—"It is well known to those who have the charge of young infants, that it is difficult to feel sure when certain movements about their mouths are really expressive; that is, when they really smile. Hence I carefully watched my own infants. One of them, at the age of forty-five days, and being at the time in a happy frame of mind, smiled; that is, the corners of the mouth were retracted, and simultaneously the eyes became decidedly bright. I observed the same thing on the following day; but on the third day the child was not quite well, and there was no trace of a smile, and this renders it probable that the previous smiles were real. Eight days subsequently, and during the next succeeding week, it was remarkable how his eyes brightened whenever he smiled, and his nose became at the same time transversely wrinkled. This was now accompanied by a little bleating noise, which perhaps represented a laugh. At the age of 113 days, these little noises, which were always made during expiration, assumed a slightly different character, and were more broken or interrupted, as in sobbing; and this was certainly incipient laughter."

In a second infant the first real smile was seen at about the same age, and in a third somewhat earlier. In this gradual acquirement, by infants, of the habit of laughing, we have a case analogous to other uses of the human frame. As practice is requisite with the ordinary movements of the body, such as walking, so it seems to be with laughing; it must grow, and if in its growth it is twisted out of form, it will never be a graceful and pleasant expression of joyous feeling.

The natural smile in children of a larger growth is interfered with by another cause. Young ladies seem to think that the glory of a woman does not lie, as of old time, in her long hair, so much as in her mouth. Modern ideas of beauty insist that the mouth must be small, therefore the owners of them must make them as small as possible. The facial efforts made to effect this purpose are prodigious. The lips are drawn in, and useless attempts are made to contract the lateral extension; while the desire to look cheerful, which naturally lengthens the mouth, fights with the antagonistic determination to keep within limits, and the result is an hysterical grin.

In a true smile the lips are parted more or less widely, with the corners of the mouth drawn backwards, as well as a little upwards, causing wrinkles to form under the eyes, and the eyes become partially closed. As a gentle smile grows into a strong one, or into a laugh, the upper lip is drawn up, and the muscles under the eyes contract, the wrinkles under the lower eyelids, and those beneath the eyes, are much strengthened and increased, and the eyebrows are slightly lowered. Now, all these natural effects of a smile are quite incompatible with large eyes and small mouths.

One of the most difficult features a photographer has to

contend with is that form of mouth which has permanently-parted lips, leaving the teeth full in view. This is an effect that seems to be becoming more prevalent in this country. An inspection of a large collection of old photographic portraits will show that it did not exist to such an extent even twenty years ago. The effect is usually not disagreeable in nature. Momentary changes of expression seem to qualify the defect, if defect it can be called; but in a photograph, when the form is permanent, and has not the aid of varied movement, the effect is not agreeable, and gives the photographer much trouble, and taxes his ingenuity to hide it. This is a case in which any attempt at smiling is best avoided, as it only tends to make matters worse.

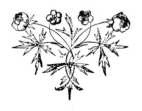

CHAPTER XVII.

LIKENESS—FAMILIAR AND OCCULT.

A SATISFACTORY resemblance to the original is a primary excellence in a portrait of any kind, taking precedence, indeed, of all other qualities. The resemblance which is thus important is that which is sufficiently familiar and striking to be recognised by the least analytic of observers, and which does not require ingenuity to discover, or argument to enforce. It should be the kind of resemblance which a child would recognise, and which must depend more on the truthful resemblance of the whole than on the perfection of any individual part.

The production of such likenesses is not so common in photography as it ought to be; and although good photography is important to the production of a good likeness, it depends less on technical excellence in the picture than on the exercise of good judgment on the part of the sitter. It is dependent also upon other matters beyond the control or knowledge of the portraitist, but in regard to which he should exercise, as far as possible, a watchful supervision. I have referred in another chapter, and now refer again, to the circumstance which professional portraitists know so well, and from which they suffer so much annoyance, such as the entire change of the ordinary costume on the part of the sitter when preparing to sit for a portrait. How often a lady who usually wears her hair plainly braided, curls it especially for the express purpose of sitting for her portrait, to the entire destruction of anything like familiarity in the resemblance! And so with other modifications in the general costume. The portraitist should suggest, wherever opportunity serves, the importance of preserving the usual and familiar appearance in the arrangement of dress, &c., in all cases where the portrait is to be prized as a likeness of the sitter, rather than preserved as a memento of some special effect of costume.

But one of the most valuable aids to familiarity of effect in a portrait is the securing of characteristic position—a thing nine times out of ten lost in the arrangement made by the portraitist. The sitter is placed in a chair, very often of unusual construction—perhaps low in the seat, possibly straight-backed, and mediæval; he is then arranged so as to bear a given relation to the position of the camera, and to the arrangement of the light; his hands are placed in approved form; his head is fixed in a rest; he is directed to gaze at a certain spot, and he is then invited to look pleasant, and sit perfectly still.

"Quiet as a stone,
Still as the silence."

He becomes at once conscious of the vital importance of the moment; if he is doubtful of his steadiness, he makes a special effort, with a look of ferocious agony, to sit perfectly still; if he is more anxious about the expression than about his steadiness, he probably puts on an insufferable smirk. In either case a portrait with nothing of familiar likeness is the result.

The shrewd and observant portraitist will do the reverse of all this, and direct his sitter to take his seat, and will then, observing the position naturally assumed before "arrangement" has commenced, with the least possible disturbance of the position, secure the general disposal of the figure, and, wherever it is possible, produce the necessary variety by moving the camera and re-arranging the light to suit the sitter, rather than arrange the sitter to suit the position of the camera and the light. The more like the interior of an ordinary sitting room the studio can be made, the more comfortable the accessories, and the less formal and exacting the arrangement of the sitter, the more familiar the likeness will probably be.

There is another important consideration, which will have weight in the minds of many, and which will frequently interfere with the familiarity of the likeness. If the question be asked, " Is it of more importance to secure a good photograph and agreeable picture, or to secure a familiar and satisfactory likeness? " many will answer that it is more important to secure a good picture; that if the photography and pictorial arrangement be good, the likeness ought to be satisfactory ; and to such an extent is this feeling carried by some, that they are literally unable to perceive or acknowledge that the likeness is bad, if the picture be good. The defect, they allege, is a want of perception in the observer; or the sitter's face is one which " does not make a striking likeness." In any case, the photography is good in all points, and there is nothing pictorially wrong, and therefore the portrait ought to be good; and, if it is not, the portraitist cannot be to blame, they fancy. I have so often insisted on the importance of artistic arrangement, and of making portraits pleasing and striking pictures, that I shall not be misunderstood, I hope, if I say that in some instances this very desire interferes with the familiarity of the likeness.

Here is a case in point in the shape of a series of portraits of an intimate friend, with every phase of whose fine and striking countenance I am familiar. He has delighted the public, counting his readers by hundreds of thousands, and made some fame and position for himself as a novelist, essayist, poet, &c.; has been photographed by many artists, each of whom has, doubtless, striven to produce an effective portrait of a man of

mark. Here are cards and whole plates by various first-rate
photographers, and of these, whilst all are more or less good
pictures, and all more or less like, there are but two which are
thoroughly characteristic and satisfactory, the chief fault in
most of them being too much striving after effect. In one we
have a profile with chin thrown up, and the whole effect self-
asserting and truculent; in another we have a standing figure,
with open book in one hand, and a finger of the other hand laid
on a page, reminding you of Mr. Chadband holding forth, as
delineated in " Bleak House "; and so on with others. These
effects were doubtless present before the camera at the moment
when the plate was impressed, and were the result of an unskilful
striving after striking effect in the pose and arrangement. Many
operators, in their desire to avoid producing the mere maps of
the face which have been so often charged on photography as
its normal product, fall into this opposite extreme of inducing
the sitter to act a part; and as very few persons are good actors,
it is not surprising that in such cases the portraits, however
excellent as pictures, are unfamiliar as likenesses. Let the
portraitist ever bear in mind that the less importance the sitter
attaches to the vital moment of exposure, the more natural will
be his expression; the fewer injunctions as to looking pleasant,
sitting still, keeping his eye fixed, &c., the less likely he will
be to look affected and simpering on the one hand, or nervous
and anxious on the other.

Besides the advantages of a quiet and natural portrait in
giving familiar likeness, it often possesses another advantage in
having certain occult traits of likeness, only discoverable under
special circumstances. This is a peculiarity of a really good
and natural photographic portrait, which to the psychologist
and physiognomist is an interesting study. How often, in a
good photographic portrait, a family likeness to a relative is
discovered which had not been apparent to anyone in the
original! How often, in the photograph of a child, is suddenly

perceived its wondrous likeness to a dead grandsire, which until that moment had never been thought of—

> " As sometimes in a dead man's face,
> To those who watch it more and more,
> A likeness, hardly seen before,
> Comes out—to some one of his race."

It is generally in the simple, unconstrained, familiar likeness that these unfamiliar or occult phases of resemblance are most present as well.

Rejlander once brought this matter of occult likeness to a very crucial test. At a country house where he was visiting there was a beautiful little girl; on the walls of the dining room was the portrait, old and cracked, of an ancestress, painted when the lady was about the age of the child. Rejlander dressed and posed the child like the ancestress, and photographed her. On the negative he imitated the cracks and defects of the old picture; he then made a negative of the picture, and when both were printed, it was difficult to say which was the ancestress and which the descendant.

Nathaniel Hawthorne, in his charming romance, "The House with Seven Gables," gives another striking illustration of this presence of occult likeness in photographs, even in a case in which the familiar or obvious likeness is wanting. The passage describing this is quoted here for the benefit of those who may not remember it. A photographer is speaking :—

" ' There is a wonderful insight in Heaven's broad and simple sunshine. While we give it credit only for depicting the merest surface, it actually brings out the secret character with a truth no painter would ever venture upon, even could he detect it. There is at least no flattery in my humble line of art. Now, here is a likeness which I have taken over and over again, and still with no better result. Yet the original wears, to common eyes, a very different expression. It would gratify me to have your judgment on this character.' He exhibited a Daguerreo-

I

type miniature in a morocco case. Phœbe merely glanced at it, and gave it back.

" ' I know the face,' she replied, ' for its stern eye has been following me about all day. It is my Puritan ancestor, who hangs yonder in the parlour. To be sure, you have found some way of copying the portrait without its black velvet cap and grey beard, and have given him a modern coat and satin cravat instead of his cloak and band. I don't think him improved by your alterations.'

" ' You would have seen other differences had you looked a little longer,' said Holgrave, laughing, yet apparently much struck. ' I can assure you that this is a modern face, and one which you will very probably meet. Now, the remarkable point is that the original wears, to the world's eye, and, for aught I know, to his most intimate friends, an exceedingly pleasant countenance, indicative of benevolence, openness of heart, seeming good humour, and other praiseworthy qualities of that cast. The sun, as you see, tells quite another story, and will not be coaxed out of it, after half a dozen patient attempts on my part. Here we have the man sly, subtle, hard, imperious; withal, cold as ice. Look at that eye. Would you like to be at its mercy? At that mouth. Could it ever smile? And yet if you could only see the benign smile of the original! It is so much the more unfortunate as he is a public character of some eminence, and the likeness was intended to be engraved.'

" ' Well, I don't wish to see it any more,' observed Phœbe, turning away her eyes. ' It is certainly very like the old portrait.' "

The Daguerreotype here tells the truth. The smiling descendant of the stern old Puritan is really a man hard, cruel, and black of heart ; and these qualities, in conjunction with the family traits of a race, persistently make themselves apparent in the picture limned by the sun, even though imperceptible to common observers of the original. The possession of these subtle peculiarities of likeness is a quality of much importance in historical portraiture, whether the history be that of individuals, of families, or of nations, and is one well worth noting and preserving. The quality can only belong to honest untouched photographs, free alike from affectation and constraint; the simple rendering of a face with a natural expression, with due attention to the best technical appliances of lighting, arrangement, exposure, and development.

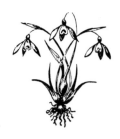

CHAPTER XVIII.

RETOUCHING.

I SHALL have nothing to say on the manipulative details of retouching. Practical information on the subject has been so often given in the journals and separate publications, that reiteration would be wearisome, as well as out of place here; but a glance at the history and progress of retouching may be both interesting and instructive. In the earliest days of photographic portraiture, retouching was not only unknown, but impossible. The exquisitely delicate surface of the Daguerreotype would not tolerate for a moment the touch of mechanical amelioration; except, indeed, so far as the process of tinting or colouring effected that end. The colours were applied in the form of an impalpable powder, and the result of their application had more the character of a stain than of applied pigments. The finest touch of water-colours was so incongruous with the delicate surface of the picture that a coarse, patchy effect was the result in all cases, no matter how skilfully applied. Curiously enough, the untouched Daguerreotype presented fewer of the crudities of texture, was less cruel in its renderings of wrinkles, freckles, and rugosities, than any later form of photographic portraiture.

On the advent of the collodion process, photographs on paper gradually superseded the Daguerreotype. At its best, the paper print fell far short of the delicacy of the silver plate, and at its worst it was often a sadly coarse, stained, smudgy affair. Now commenced the practice of retouching on the print to remove technical defects, and ameliorate, as far as possible, what appeared to be inherent photographic shortcomings. Then followed those abominations consisting of photographic prints entirely worked up in Indian ink or sepia, the photographic image being generally destroyed, and a hard, unnatural, badly-drawn monochrome presented in its place. None of these methods were effective against freckles. Then it struck photographers that the proper thing to touch up was the model, and all kinds of powders and cosmetics were brought into play, until sitters did not think they were being properly treated if their faces and hair were not powdered until they looked like a ghastly mockery of the clown in a pantomine. There are sitters even now who will not believe they are being taken in the truly foreign manner—"where the light is so clear, you know"—if the photographer does not dust their heads a little by way of throwing dust in their eyes.

The idea of retouching on the negative very tardily dawned on the photographic community, and it came slowly into general practice, until about the year 1867, when its uses were generally recognised, and its abuses, of course, quickly followed. The removal of blemishes like stains and pinholes in the negative was customary. It is probable, moreover, that for many years before the practice of retouching had become general, some photographers manipulated their negatives considerably, carefully preserving their practice in this way as a secret. A case may be remembered, many years ago, at a photographic exhibition, when the fine contributions of a very able photographer were challenged by another portraitist as being retouched. The response to this was an offer to permit the prints to be sponged with water. The challenger insisted that the stippling was manifest beyond question when the prints were examined by a magnifying glass. The production of unmounted prints with precisely similar gradation, which was not removed by sponging, seemed to settle the matter by deciding that there could be no retouching, the negatives never being suspected.

There can be no doubt now—and if there were any I can set it at rest, for I have seen many of the negatives—that the exquisite vignettes of the late T. R. Williams, which were the admiration and despair of the photographers of thirty years ago, owed much of their beauty to very judicious retouching on the negative, added to the great care and almost fastidious taste of that admirable photographer. Retouching, used at a time when the process was not suspected, gave these portraits a superiority over others that it is now almost impossible to believe.

The use of lead pencils for retouching upon the negative first rendered this operation possible as a popular process. Stippling upon a varnished surface with wet pigments was a difficult process, requiring great manipular skill, and few of those possessing that skill were familiar with the requirements of negative retouching, in which the degree of opacity or translucency of each touch is of more importance than its appearance by reflected light. The first suggestion for the use of lead pencil for this purpose came from Germany in 1866. Since that time the system has steadily progressed. Its use in any degree has been strongly condemned by photographic purists as a departure from the truth as it is in photography, and, curiously enough, one of its most staunch opponents was one who was unrivalled in the artistic manipulation of the negative in printing operations— the late O. G. Rejlander. In the earlier years of negative retouching, photographers would confess its use with apology and hesitation. It soon, however, acquired a firm foothold in the studio of every portraitist, and the skilled retoucher was indispensable. In this country the legitimacy of the process, *per se*, is no longer discussed, but is, by general consent, tacitly admitted.

Excess is, of course, condemned as inartistic, untrue, and unwise, even by those who most egregiously overstep the fair line of legitimacy. Photographers occasionally discuss the subject still. Even those who object to its use artistically defend the practice as necessary to meet the demands of the public, every individual of whom, whilst professing to require the simple truth of photography without retouching, invariably protests against receiving a portrait in which the retoucher's art had not been more or less employed. Others hope that the mania for retouching will run its course; that unreasonable excess will bring reaction.

Where excess of retouching not only levels all ages, and makes it difficult to distinguish the portrait of the grandmother from the pretty girl of twenty, who is so like her; and where it destroys the texture of the flesh, and substitutes that of chiselled marble, its evil is beyond dispute. Where it is or may be used for fraud, the evil is still more lamentable. Some years ago there was a case in which a portrait from an untouched and somewhat harsh negative, and one from a fine negative of the same sitter, very carefully retouched, so as to remove lines, wrinkles, or rugosities, were prepared for exhibiting in court, the latter as showing the state of an individual before a misfortune for which he claimed damages, and the former as showing the distressing effect produced upon his health by the misfortune for which damages were claimed. It is probable that the two portraits were produced in the order of time claimed for them; but the misused art of the retoucher might make either of them tell the tale either of decrepitude or vigorous health.

The common complaint against excessive retouching has much less justification than is supposed. That which is frequently described as excess in retouching is less the result of excess than of ignorance. It is not that there is too much of the pencil, but that it is applied in the wrong place. A very little unskilful retouching will remove the texture of the flesh, and leave that of stone; will remove the expression of a living face, and leave that of a mask; whilst the same amount of retouching applied with knowledge and intelligence would have retained the texture of flesh, removing only the temporary and accidental blemishes and the exaggerations of photography which interfered with truth and beauty; would have given fuller effect to a fine expression, or subdued a suspicion of frowning or weariness by delicate touches applied in the right place. Photographers, innocent alike of the structure of the human face and of any knowledge of drawing, unhesitatingly retouch negatives without the slightest idea that any other qualification than a photographic eye and a steady hand is necessary. They neatly fill up wrinkles and scars and soften shadows, until they produce a face almost as smooth and quite as expressionless as a billiard ball. And, what is more, they are proud of the result!

Retouching, then, may now be included amongst the legitimate processes of photography. That it is unfortunately open to abuse, and that the abuse of it in ignorant eyes is beautiful, cannot be helped. There is a class of people who never care to refer to nature. With them, to be smooth and soft is to be beautiful. They may not care to have their own faces enamelled, but they do not object to the highly-retouched fraud which represents them as marble, and will complacently offer it to you as a portrait of themselves.

Retouching is legitimate when it does not falsify nature; it should be used only to aid the well-known shortcoming of photography. In nature we scarcely see a freckle on the face if we do not look closely for it; in the negative the freckle is represented by a hole which prints much darker than the freckle appears in nature; it is legitimate to fill up this hole so that the result may the better represent nature. A warm shadow or reflected light may come out darker than in nature: these places may be aided and strengthened. A high-light may fall short of the sparkle of the original; this may also be strengthened.

To know when to leave off should be the aim of the retoucher.

He is the best artist who knows when his work is done. If as much time and thought were taken to get perfect negatives as is spent in correcting imperfections, the retoucher's art would come nearly to an end.

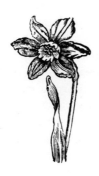

CHAPTER XIX.

HINTS TO SITTERS.

MANY photographers have published little pamphlets and circulars addressed to their patrons to teach them how to dress and what to do when they go to sit for their portraits. They are first told how to make appointments, then follow instructions what to do "when you visit us." Some of the advice must be quite appalling to nervous sitters. The injunction to keep steady if you want "a thing of beauty," and not to object to anything, but to "place yourself entirely in our operator's hands," is so disquieting that it is scarcely compensated for by the promise that if you do you will be rewarded with the best results. What can give a sitter a more serious impression of the profound nature of the operation than the following :—"Do not object to the head-rest; it is quite essential for keeping the sitter steady after being posed. It is more difficult to sit steady than you would think, and remember the slighest movement spoils the picture." The information is right enough, but why bother the sitter with it? You are not to come flushed and panting, or your face will come out black. You are to come in a pleasant frame of mind, because "the reflex of the mental condition is unavoidably indexed on the face." You must choose your dress and jewellery with discrimination, and as the operator orders. You are not to stare, but may wink—a liberty for which the sitter must feel grateful. You are not to pile your hair on the top of the head, and you may introduce curls occasionally with advantage. Powder is recommended to give detail which would be otherwise wanted, but how it does so is rather puzzling. And then comes the inevitable condemnation of some colours for dresses, such as blue, lilac, and lavender, and recommendation of others, such as black, claret, scarlet, pea green, yellow, crimson, slate, and especially black silk and black lace.

All this is better left alone. To print all these directions, even if they were the reverse of very foolish, is to give the operation of sitting for a portrait such importance that the victims will be inclined to think very seriously of it, *and look like it*. It is my experience that the more a sitter is prepared, the worse he sits. The more he *doesn't* know what you are going to do with him the better will be his portrait. Of course it does happen sometimes that a lady comes most unsuitably dressed— say in stiff white material, spotted or barred with black velvet, or in loud checks. It is much better to tell her quietly that the dress is unsuitable, and get her to postpone the sitting, than to give her printed directions what to do which only help to confuse her. Nearly the only stipulation the photographer should make with a lady sitter is, that she *should come dressed like herself*. This is important, for ladies are sometimes inclined to make experiments and try an unaccustomed costume. If they come " as guys, or in disguise "—if I may quote from one of the jealously-guarded rules of the Solar Club—they cannot expect to look like themselves. Photographers are suffering much from ladies' dress at the present time. I don't mean that it is ugly— I have said my say on that matter in a former chapter—but from the make, or cut, or fit of the dress. The operator can sometimes get rid of a mass of bulbous ugliness by recommending a vignette head; but it is in this kind of picture that the present difficulty arises. The dresses are made perfectly plain in the body, and it is not in nature, to say nothing of the dressmaker's art, that wrinkles should not show in a part that is constantly moving. It seems to be a point of the first consideration that no wrinkles shall show, and that the shoulders shall be as smooth as marble. Everything has to be sacrificed to this one fad. Ease and grace are disregarded; but the shoulders must be thrown back to keep the dress tight. I should say that at the present there are more re-sittings to get rid of these insignificant but perfectly natural wrinkles than from any other cause.

There are some gentle hints that the photographer may very properly suggest. People often come in from the country to have their hair cut, to go to the dentist, and to be photographed. I think they may be gently warned against the absurdity of combining these operations in one visit; but if they must take place on the same day, the photographer may fairly ask to have first show.

The photographer ought to be able to make presentable pictures out of any subject brought to him, but there are some things to which he may reasonably take objection; others that he once upon a time refused to have anything to do with, are often now his great delight. At one time white dresses were strongly objected to for ladies and children, but now the judicious photographer will welcome them with pleasure. He has so improved his methods of lighting that an object that once came out as a mere blank mass of white paper can now be made to take the most delicate and subtle shades. A white dress, lighted from behind, usually comes well, especially if it is not straight from the wash; a dress that has been worn some time always looks better in a photograph than a new one.

There are other hints—and broad ones, too—that may be given to sitters without going to the extreme length of sending them a pamphlet on the subject. For instance, a hint may be given that a little dog is a very objectionable animal in a studio; that when he is taking a portrait the operator has something more important to think of than dogs, and cannot be responsible for their lives if they run between his legs. Another hint has sometimes to be given that you cannot talk over business matters with the sitter's friends while you are thinking about the pose and exposure; and I have known it to be necessary to suggest to a sitter or his friend that he must not smoke in the studio. There have been rare occasions when I have gone even further.

The strongest hint I ever saw made to sitters was printed in large letters on a screen, at which the sitter was made to look when the exposure was made. It ran to this effect:—"You are expected to pay at the time of sitting!" There was a mingling of business with art in this that could not be considered as an aid to expression, and which I never could approve of.

Another useful hint to a sitter who is troublesome in that difficult matter of re-sittings, is that the negatives and prints of all portraits not approved are invariably destroyed before the re-sitting. This circumvents those unreasonable people whose only object—which they have to gain by aid of untruths—is to have a large and varied collection to select from.

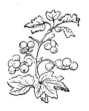

CHAPTER XX.

HOW TO SHOW PHOTOGRAPHS.

A GOOD photograph badly mounted is like a jewel ill-set, and a great part of its beauty is lost. No artist should be indifferent to the manner and style in which his work is shown to the public. A glance round the Royal Academy Exhibitions will show that more attention is being given year by year to the suitability of the frame to the picture which it encloses. Many artists design their own. A few hints and suggestions on the subject may not be out of place. We will commence with a consideration of how to show a card portrait.

Nothing fanciful should be allowed in the mounting of a carte-de-visite. This card should be plain, either white, or, what is perhaps better, a very light buff or cream colour. Pinks, the various shades of mauve, and cold greys are most unsuitable; the thick black and chocolate mounts, with gold bevelled edges, effectively show up the photograph, the one thing against them being that their thickness prevents their use in albums. There are green cards of this kind that do not harmonize with the picture. The margin should not be wider than one-sixteenth of an inch, with a quarter or five-sixteenths of an inch at the bottom, upon which it is allowable for the photographer to print his name, very faintly, in black or brown ink; but to print the name large, or in staring red letters, not only shows bad taste,

but detracts from the effect of the picture. Printed lines round
the edge of the card are wrong, so are round corners; but when
the lines and round corners are combined, they appear to have
entered into a conspiracy to spoil the picture, and generally
succeed, however good it may be. I hold it to be as necessary
to have the photographer's name on the back of the card—
always supposing the picture is not a copy—as it is to have a
picture on the front; but the name must not be set forth in a
glaring design, full of curlycues and flourishes, but in a modest
and quiet fashion; not as though you were ashamed of it, but
without any advertising dash. A thin card is better than a
thick one; it feels better if well rolled, and does not fill up the
book so much as a thick one would.

To cabinet pictures and larger sizes mounted with narrow
margins the same general rules will apply, except that the
margins should be proportionately wider.

As to the framing of cartes-de-visite and cabinets, there is
such an infinite variety of devices provided for this purpose by
manufacturers, that it is difficult to offer any advice on the subject. However, you may take this as a general rule: do not
overframe. Let us degenerate into anecdote. Some years ago
I was present at the unpacking of some of the pictures sent to
one of our exhibitions. There was one case brought in with
difficulty—it was enormous, it filled the hall. I said to the
porter, before it was opened, "We must have a few tons of very
fine pictures here." Other cases were neglected; we opened
the large one. The parturient mountain brought forth a little
mouse: the case was full of most tremendous specimens of the
carver and gilder's art, but there was very little art of any other
kind. Amongst others, there was one large moulded frame,
several inches in depth, and with a gilt matt inside; it con-
tained seven cartes-de-visite of the cameo form—that was all—
reminding one of Falstaff's halfpennyworth of bread to an intolerable deal of sack. I have entered more fully into this part

of the subject, because there is evidence in exhibitions of a great attempt to hide bad work in gorgeous frames. An oil painting will carry a heavy frame, but a photograph, except it is large and dark, will not. It should rather be classed in this respect as a water-colour drawing, which should never be smothered in carving and gold.

To return to cartes and cabinets and small sizes for a few moments. Heavy plush frames in every variety of gaudy colour have been very fashionable for some time, the unique hideousness of which fairly surpasses anything ever invented in the way of unfitness. The brightly-coloured plush is allowed to be in contact with the photograph; there is no gilt flat or bead to prevent the injurious contrast, and the general impression, on a first look at a photograph thus gorgeously framed, is that the poor little thing is a disgrace to its surroundings. Now this is a reversal of the intention of a frame, which should be to set off and benefit the picture.

In the same way, the very elaborate albums with sometimes beautifully designed and coloured leaves, forming borders for the photographs, destroy by their beauty the very thing they are designed to show off and honour. The object of an album is to hold portraits or other photographs, and it should be designed so as to assist the effect of those photographs in every way. They should be plain and good. I do not object to a line round the apertures, but I prefer them without. The apertures should be square or oval, or both; but fanciful shapes, such as the dome and cushion, should be rejected.

Velvet frames of a modest colour, such as marone, are good, especially for finished pictures on opal, either in monochrome or colour; but the velvet must always be divided from the photograph with at least half-an-inch of gold.

A landscape is best mounted in or on a light buff mount, with a margin from three to four inches, according to size, without gilt lines, and enclosed in a frame not more than two or three inches in depth. A one-inch bead is sufficient for sizes under 10 by 8. A running ornament round the frame is not objectionable, so that it is neat, and if there are no heavy corners. If you send frames with elaborate corners to exhibitions, you are pretty sure to get them back in more pieces than is desirable, and they will not get good places. In the first place, it is impossible, in arranging an exhibition, to think much of the preservation of the frames ; in the next, heavy frames are put aside for further consideration, however good the pictures may be they contain. But, as usual, there is a lower depth, the Oxford frame. However anxious the "hangers" may be to do their best, they draw the line at the Oxford frame ; they can keep their tempers till they come to these sprawling abominations, and then "the worst inn's worst room" is nothing to the place these are consigned to, if a place bad enough can be found. These "hints to exhibitors" are worth remembering.

Of late years a great deal of oak, principally in light tints, has been used for framing photographs. The patterns are usually unobjectionable, and some of them, when the flutings and other parts are gilt, are quite beautiful, and fit for drawing-room use. An inch flat of light oak with an inch of gilt beading make an admirable exhibition frame. It is cheap, looks well, and defies the horny-handed porters to scratch or destroy it.

Large and dark portraits are best framed close up in gilt or dark frames two or three inches in depth, with a broad gilt flat. Vignettes are better in a lighter style of framing ; oval mounts, light buff or warm grey, in simple gilt frames.

A plain photograph should never be exhibited in the same room with oil-pictures or water-colour drawings. Due attention should be paid to the colour of the paper of the wall on which photographs are hung. The pattern should be delicate and unpronounced, of a geometrical or conventional design, without any staring contrasts of colours. The tone of colour may be of a dull red or chocolate, or, what is perhaps better, a sage green.

In showing a coloured photograph, the light should be so arranged as to fall upon it from the direction in which it was allowed to fall upon the picture while the artist was at work upon it— almost always from the left. When the picture is viewed with the light from the right, all the inequalities of the surface of the paper are seen, and the work appears coarse and slovenly. The reason of this is, that the artist, in working up his picture, fills up with stippling all the inequalities he sees; these inequalities, however fine the surface of the paper may be, are caused by the grain of the paper, also by the minutely different thicknesses of the colour he applies, and it would be utterly impossible to finish a picture that would appear as well with the light one way as the other.

In their useful little volume, "Painting Popularly Explained," Messrs. Timbs and Gullick recommend : " For water-colour paintings it is especially important that the frames should not be heavy or too profusely ornamented. A massive frame will almost destroy the effect of delicate work in water-colours. Burnishing small points of the frame is, however, from the greater vivacity of water-colours, less objectionable than when the frame is intended to enclose an oil picture. The glass of the frame should not touch the face of the painting. The 'mount,' or margin intervening between the water-colour painting and its frame, is almost invariably white; though it might not unfrequently with great advantage be tinted, especially if the painting is merely a vignette. For all delicate work light in tone, a paper mount is preferable; and for such, a simple gold bead frame with a gold edge to the mount next the picture is very suitable. But more powerfully and intensely-coloured water paintings, especially if warm in tone, might often be rendered far more effective and harmonious by substituting a gold mount."

Large oil pictures are chiefly exhibited without glass, but coloured oil portraits, except the very largest, most certainly look richer, more finely finished, and fuller in colour under glass.

Glass is also a great protection to the picture. " The frequent assertion that glass interferes with the effect of oil pictures," says Ruskin, " is wholly irrelevant. If a painting cannot be seen through glass, it cannot be seen through its own varnish. Any position which renders the glass offensive by its reflection will in like manner make the glaze of the surface of the picture visible instead of the colour. The inconvenience is less distinct, there being often only a feeble glimmer on the varnish, when there would be a vivid flash on the glass; but the glimmer is quite enough to prevent the true colours being seen; while there is this advantage in the glass, that it tells the spectator when he cannot see, whereas the glimmer of the varnish often passes, with an inattentive observer, for a feeble part of the real painting, and he does not try to get into a better position."

The permanency of a silver print—and, to a less extent, all other pictures on paper, whether photograph, engraving, or water-colour drawing—depends on the way in which it is framed and kept. The frame should be air-tight and well protected from damp. Perhaps nothing, after they are mounted, is so destructive to photographs as damp. It mildews carbon prints, and quickly insists on silver prints fading away. The air should be rigidly excluded. It is common to see the back of a frame pasted up, but rare to find the glass pasted in. This should always be done. Every possible precaution should be taken to avoid damp walls. This is so necessary that I never think any walls are safe that are not made damp-proof, for which purpose I prefer a lining of Willesden paper—a material which, by-the-bye, is useful for many photographic purposes.

This subject is open to much expansion, but with these few hints I will leave it.

CHAPTER XXI.

THE ITINERANT PAINTER.

CLOSELY connected with the subject of portrait photography, and of great interest to the professional photographer, is that of the ownership of the negative and future orders.

When a well-established photographer takes a portrait, he looks for his profit, not only to the sum he receives for the first order for copies, but to the contingent potentialities which may arise from the possession of the negatives, and to that end he goes to a great deal of trouble and expense in cataloguing and storing them. Of course the great proportion of these negatives are never wanted again, and are an incumbrance; but all professional photographers know that there is so good a demand for copies from old negatives, that they find it to their interest to keep all they take, and to print prominently on the back of their cards, " All negatives are preserved. Copies or enlargements of this portrait can always be had." Talking on this subject the other day to a photographer, he said, pointing to a beautifully finished enlargement, " Here is an instance. One day, some years ago, a shabby old gentleman came into the reception room, and said he wanted his portrait taken. He was shown specimens, but he said they were all too dear; he could only afford half-a-guinea, and if I liked to do it for that sum he should be glad to have it done. I liked the appearance of the old man, who looked poor but respectable, so as a kind of charity I took a negative of him. I was so pleased with him, that I offered to send him a dozen copies without charge, but he would not accept this offer, saying he had to drive a bargain sometimes but he could pay his way, and paid his half-guinea. I found afterwards I had entertained an angel—a business angel —unawares, for I have done nearly £300 from that negative since. The fine old gentleman died soon afterwards, and then I found he was a famous manufacturer, and that the portrait I had taken had a peculiar expression in the eyes of his friends, that had never been got before in any portrait he had had taken, and the orders for enlargements poured in, and still continue." This is, of course, an extreme instance of the value of a kept negative; but "back orders," as they are sometimes called, are so constant that many photographers who keep careful statistics of their business can tell to a few pounds how much their old negatives will bring in every year. Then they constitute one of the bases on which businesses are valued—in short, they are property.

It is a constant complaint of photographers that they are always open to, or suffering from, the attacks of those who want to rob them of this property. There is a class of people who misuse the great name of artist—as, indeed, for the matter of that, some photographers do, by applying it to themselves—who go round the country, and, by means of introduction or impudence, obtain orders for portraits, usually enlargements painted from photographs. As they never take an original portrait themselves, they require the negative, and use every means, fair or foul, to obtain it, and are usually successful. The method of proceeding is something like this. The father of a family has been dead a short time; the itinerant hears of this, and before she has had time to apply to a photographer, gets an introduction to the widow. A great part of his success in his business depends on fluent and persuasive speaking, and the lady is soon induced to order a portrait of her late husband. And some of the "tramps" are so pressing and plausible, that they compel orders against the will, or certainly against the calmer reason, of their victims. When the order is booked, they ask to see a portrait of the husband, and take down the name of the photographer. They usually get the widow to write for the loan of the negative, taking great care to explain that no injury shall happen to it, and that he is sure the photographer will be delighted to lend it to a brother artist, especially as it is of no further use to himself. Perhaps the photographer reluctantly consents, seeing no way out of it; or he more properly and wisely refuses to lend the negative. In this case the itinerant brings more pressure to bear, showing to his patron how selfish and inconsiderate the photographer is in preventing her having a splendid portrait of her husband now there is such a fine opportunity. The result is that the unfortunate photographer is placed on the horns of a dilemma; if he consent to lend the negative, he loses the benefits for which he has speculatively kept it for years; and if he refuse, he runs the risk of losing an old and good customer.

There are grades, even in this low class of art. There is the "perfect gentleman"—that class of gentlemen who are never seen without their gloves, who select a suitable town and take a good house or grand apartments, and work all the country round. Here is one of the princes of the profession who occasionally gets as much as £100 for a picture. This practitioner can afford, and sometimes does pay, the photographer for the use of a negative, but he often induces him to join in risky practices that are certain to bring him into disrepute with his patrons. For nstance, amongst the photographer's specimens he will see a fine-looking man or a beautiful woman, and, first ascertaining if the game is worth the candle—that is, if their proposed victim is rich and amiable, or able to pay and timid—he paints his picture, sends it to the victim beautifully framed, explaining as his reason for painting it that the head was so fine that he really could not help trying to do it justice, and he thinks he has succeeded. No mention of price is made in this first experiment. He probably gets it back with a letter of thanks, and a civil word or two about it being very well done, &c. Then begins a series of puttings on of the screw, running sometimes at the last to the most unscrupulous proceedings, until the victim succumbs—and pays. It is astonishing what a quantity of orders these men will get, until at last they make the town too hot to hold them, and move on to another.

These itinerant painters are not all of the male persuasion; a good many are ladies, ranging from the old miniature painter—the Miss Le Creevys are not yet extinct—down through students who have failed in original art, to the merest tinters. I hear of them from all quarters, and am often requested to give advice as to what is the best manner of treating them. This is very difficult to give; different circumstances require different treatment; but in most cases the best policy would be to refuse to have anything to do with the poachers. It should be easy to explain to a client that a photographer ought not to be expected to give up the fruits of his foresight and care, that he could scarcely afford to warehouse negatives for the benefit of others, and above all—and he must show this—that he can produce as good a picture as the itinerant at the same price.

Whether one photographer should occasionally lend a negative to another is quite a different question. I am inclined to think there are many occasions when they should oblige one another—it may be for their reciprocal advantage; but I can see nothing to be gained by encouraging those who prowl about the country trying to get work out of the hands of those to whom it legitimately belongs.

CHAPTER XXII.

THE EDUCATION OF A PHOTOGRAPHER.

I HAVE often been asked the question, " What is the best course of study for a young man who has determined to devote his life to photography as a profession ? "

This is a wide subject; let us endeavour to reduce it to some practical form.

The earliest photographers took to the art as a business after having been trained to follow some other path in life. Those who had received a commercial training were best suited for the business part of photography—a not unimportant part, it must be owned—but those who passed an apprenticeship to chemistry had a great advantage over others as far as the working of processes was concerned, and those who had the benefit of an artistic education were in the best position for using the young art-science as a method of making pictures, which, after all, is the great end and aim of photography.

But in those days art training was not thought so much of as it is in our own. Where one student learnt to draw then, a hundred learn to draw now. There was no regular art teaching at that time ; now the Government is alive to the necessity of every boy and girl knowing something of drawing, and there are nearly a million of students attending the schools of art spread all over the kingdom, without taking into account the other millions who learn the rudiments of art in Board schools and from private teachers.

That art was at so low an ebb when photography was given to the world is one of the causes why it was so long in being recognised as an art—there were no artists.

The young photographer does now, after a fashion, serve an apprenticeship to his future business, but it is a poor affair, instituted more for the purpose of supplying the master with labour at low wages than for the education of the apprentice. He is bound for a term of years to serve his master in return for instruction in the art and mystery of photography. Practically, he gets a superficial knowledge of printing, and that is all. It would be safe to say he never gets into the studio, and seldom into the developing room. He learns nothing of the higher branches of the art of which printing is a small, if important, fraction. There are some photographers, it is true, who take a higher kind of apprentice, in this case called a pupil. The pupil, because he pays a premium instead of receiving small wages, gets taught a little more than the apprentice; he is taught how to take a negative, and if the photographer is very conscientious, he will show him how to light a head in the orthodox way; but he seldom gets a chance of practising his art on a sitter. And, indeed, I do not see how any photographer who has any respect for his art could turn his work over to a pupil. The result is that the student finds that if he is to get the education which will enable him to achieve the highest aims, he must help himself.

We will now consider those special studies which will be of most use to him in his profession.

The technicalities belonging to the science and the practice of photography have always had teachers, and are now easily mastered; indeed, a very profound knowledge of chemistry and optics is not required by the practical photographer; he only wants sufficient knowledge of this kind to enable him to understand the materials with which he works—nay, I will go further, although I know there are many who will not agree with me: I believe that a profound knowledge of the *science* of photography either in some way cramps the artistic faculty, or, what is more probable, shows an order of mind to some extent inimical to a feeling for art; both faculties are very rarely found to exist in the same person.

Sufficient facilities, then, exist to enable the student to obtain all the knowledge of the technics of photography that may be desirable; it is the picture-making power of his art, its capacity for producing pictorial results, results that can be exhibited— and, I may add, sold—which is oftenest neglected, but should be the photographer's chief study if he is to put the art to its natural use.

There are still those, as there were in the early days, who are so much fascinated with the scientific aspects of the art that they wonder "what photographers want with pictures." These enthusiasts are worthy of all respect; they are the experimenters, the inventors and modifiers of processes; to these we are indebted for the art itself; but I am speaking to those who do not want to invent, but who are content to use the processes they find ready to their hands, just as a painter or sculptor would take paint or clay to show of what excellent results the processes are capable.

First and foremost of the special studies necessary to the photographer, because it is the one thing on which all art is based, is drawing. I do not mean that the student need become a painter, or even a skilled draughtsman; but he must acquire sufficient facility in the use of the pencil to enable him, when he conceives a picture, to make a sketch of it, so as to have his arrangement of lines and distribution of light and shade before him. If he sees an effect of chiaroscuro, or of grouping, a beautiful pose, or a picturesque suggestion which he may wish to reproduce with the camera, he should have the power of preserving memoranda of these effects. But drawing now is considered almost of as much importance as reading, writing, and arithmetic, and is taught in all schools that are not hopelessly behind the age, so I need not dwell on the subject.

The student should not omit to acquire some knowledge of colour as applied to photographs, a branch of art which, in its technical details, differs considerably from painting. " Harmonious Colouring as Applied to Photographs," a new edition of which, almost entirely re-written, has just been published by Mr. Newman, 24, Soho Square, is the best treatise on the subject, if not the only one now in print.

The study of art in its most comprehensive sense is, doubtless, the work of a lifetime ; but there are one or two initial truths which should be clearly understood, and thoroughly impressed on the mind of the student. First, that very little of art can be *taught*. Second, that the chief portions of art which can be taught consist in tolerably definite and simple rules and principles easily understood and remembered, and not difficult to apply. These rules are to art what grammar is to literature. They will no more enable the painter to paint a Transfiguration than grammar taught Shakespeare how to write Hamlet ; but neither the great picture nor the great poem could have been produced without, on the one hand, a knowledge of composition, and, on the other, an acquaintance with the construction of the English language. And third, that after the mastering of certain rules, art study chiefly consists in constant observation and appreciation of the beauties of nature and art, and in attempts to realise in practice these beauties, aided by the rules and principles before acquired.

First.—Thompson, in his " Outlines of the Necessary Laws of Thought," says, " The whole of every *science* may be made the subject of teaching. Not so with *art;* much of it is not teachable." This arises from the fact that so much of art, especially in its higher aspects, belongs to feeling rather than to knowledge. It can be educed, developed, cultivated, but not communicated. To some minds, art education would be impossible except in a very small degree; but I will not dwell on this fact, as none are likely to commence the study of art without some inclination towards it, from which may be further assumed the capacity in a greater or less degree; and, admitting fully the existence of different degrees of natural ability, I protest strongly against the cant which relies on genius rather than on effort. Nothing except genius is denied to well-directed labour. But, admitting all this, I wish again to enforce the idea that much of art which can be learned by the student does not consist in lessons which can be taught by the teacher. The knowledge of the laws which govern production can be taught, but the faculty of producing cannot be imparted. That student has advanced little indeed in art culture who has not gone very frequently, both in his conception and his appreciation, if not in production, of art excellence, far beyond anything which could be definitely taught in any series of rules or lessons on the subject. My object in enforcing this position is to induce the student to depend more on his own sedulous self-culture than on the number of his lessons, or the skill of his teacher.

Second.—That portion of art which can be taught consists chiefly of rules and principles readily accessible, tolerably simple, and not difficult to understand and apply. The rules for the painter relate to drawing, colour, composition, and chiaroscuro. Of drawing I have already spoken, and colour is of comparatively little importance to the photographer, inasmuch as at present this great element in art is not one of the powers over which he has control. It is chiefly to a study of composition and chiaroscuro that the student must direct his attention. Here he will find much that is definite clearly reduced to rule, and which can be acquired from the teacher or the book. It is unfortunate that no complete and comprehensive book has been written on these subjects; but there are various elementary works from

which the necessary instructions can be gained. Howard's
"Sketcher's Manual" and "Imitative Art" are easily understood. Burnet's works on "Composition" and "Light and
Shade" are excellent. If I might mention my own works, I
may say that in "Pictorial Effect in Photography" I have
collected all that I thought would be of use to the photographer
on both subjects, and have repeated the rules of composition
and chiaroscuro more briefly in "Picture Making by Photography." Let the student master the principles and acquire
the rules at the very threshold of his art career, for here he is
on firm ground, as all that relates to the arrangement of lines
and tones can be tolerably clearly stated. It is the fashion now
with some artists and writers on art to deride rules, and, soaring
into a region of æsthetic ecstacy, become lost in a cloud of
words. Let not the student fear art rules where they relate to
subjects which can be clearly expressed and practically illustrated. That cant which believes in genius rather than work
generally repudiates rule and law, and affects to despise those
rules without which the greatest geniuses would feel crippled
instead of the reverse. Rules which have been observed from
the earliest times—rules which guided the hand of Michael
Angelo in the realisation of his grandest imaginings, and of
Raphael in every line he drew. It has been asked, "What do
the great artists care about rules? Their genius carries them
above such trammels." But such is not the fact ; a great artist
adds a knowledge of fundamental principles to his other powers,
and the more power he has, the greater use he makes of rules—
and the less he shows he has done so.

Third.—After mastering those things which can be reduced
to definite rules or clearly stated principles, art study chiefly
consists in observation and practice, in which the knowledge
gained is perpetually applied. This is the kind of study which,
with the artist, has no termination, and in which he acquires
that more exalted knowledge which cannot be so well put into

words as expressed in work, which often transcends, whilst it never opposes, law. This study the photographer should be pursuing whenever he visits a gallery of pictures, and marks in what the beauty of each consists, and how it is produced. The portrait photographer, after he has studied the rules to which I have referred, would find it greatly to his advantage to make an exhaustive study and analysis of the contents of the National Portrait Gallery. He would find here examples of the portraiture of this country for several centuries; he should then visit the National Gallery, and compare the works of the old masters of the Continental Schools: note the grace of Corregio, the dignity of Titian and Vandyck, and the magic of Rembrandt. He should then argue out with himself, with the assistance of his previous studies, the causes of these great qualities. Then let him try to reproduce these beauties in his own work. Let him test every picture he takes by the knowledge he possesses, rigorously criticising his own work, first ascertaining whether it conforms to the lower technical conditions which can be reduced to rule, and then bringing it to the higher tribunal of æsthetic excellence, and ascertain what of expression, intention, and poetry it possesses.

Ask a cultivated artist how he acquired his art-knowledge, and he will feel for a moment puzzled, and will next be tempted to say that·it is chiefly a matter of intuition; that he possessed natural taste. He has, of course, studied the rules of art; but he feels such a disposition between his perception and feeling of art and its beauties, and the meagreness of the rules he was taught, that he is tempted to fall back, especially if he has an illogical mind, on this idea of taste. The young student must distrust this vague thing called taste, and acquire the more certain culture which comes from study and patience. If the artist who has been thus questioned has a logical mind, his retrospective glance over the course of his study brings him finally to a period when he knows nothing of art, and when he only felt vaguely after it. He next acquired the knowledge which could be taught, and then proceeded to apply that; and it is by observation and patience, based on the half-forgotten rules, which have now almost become instincts, that he has acquired that art culture which makes his judgment certain both in appreciation and production.

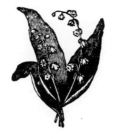

PIPER & CARTER, PRINTERS, 5, FURNIVAL STREET, HOLBORN, LONDON, E.C.

THE LITERATURE OF PHOTOGRAPHY
AN ARNO PRESS COLLECTION

Anderson, A. J. **The Artistic Side of Photography in Theory and Practice.** London, 1910

Anderson, Paul L. **The Fine Art of Photography.** Philadelphia and London, 1919

Beck, Otto Walter. **Art Principles in Portrait Photography.** New York, 1907

Bingham, Robert J. **Photogenic Manipulation.** Part I, 9th edition; Part II, 5th edition. London, 1852

Bisbee, A. **The History and Practice of Daguerreotype.** Dayton, Ohio, 1853

Boord, W. Arthur, editor. **Sun Artists** (Original Series). Nos. I-VIII. London, 1891

Burbank, W. H. **Photographic Printing Methods.** 3rd edition. New York, 1891

Burgess, N. G. **The Photograph Manual.** 8th edition. New York, 1863

Coates, James. **Photographing the Invisible.** Chicago and London, 1911

The Collodion Process and the Ferrotype: Three Accounts, 1854-1872. New York, 1973

Croucher, J. H. and Gustave Le Gray. **Plain Directions for Obtaining Photographic Pictures.** Parts I, II, & III. Philadelphia, 1853

The Daguerreotype Process: Three Treatises, 1840-1849. New York, 1973

Delamotte, Philip H. **The Practice of Photography.** 2nd edition. London, 1855

Draper, John William. **Scientific Memoirs.** London, 1878

Emerson, Peter Henry. **Naturalistic Photography for Students of the Art.** 1st edition. London, 1889

*Emerson, Peter Henry. **Naturalistic Photography for Students of the Art.** 3rd edition. *Including* The Death of Naturalistic Photography, London, 1891. New York, 1899

Fenton, Roger. **Roger Fenton, Photographer of the Crimean War.** With an Essay on his Life and Work by Helmut and Alison Gernsheim. London, 1954

Fouque, Victor. **The Truth Concerning the Invention of Photography:** Nicéphore Niépce—His Life, Letters and Works. Translated by Edward Epstean from the original French edition, Paris, 1867. New York, 1935

Fraprie, Frank R. and Walter E. Woodbury. **Photographic Amusements Including Tricks and Unusual or Novel Effects Obtainable with the Camera.** 10th edition. Boston, 1931

Gillies, John Wallace. **Principles of Pictorial Photography.** New York, 1923

Gower, H. D., L. Stanley Jast, & W. W. Topley. **The Camera As Historian.** London, 1916

Guest, Antony. **Art and the Camera.** London, 1907

Harrison, W. Jerome. **A History of Photography Written As a Practical Guide and an Introduction to Its Latest Developments.** New York, 1887

Hartmann, Sadakichi (Sidney Allan). **Composition in Portraiture.** New York, 1909

Hartmann, Sadakichi (Sidney Allan). **Landscape and Figure Composition.** New York, 1910

Hepworth, T. C. **Evening Work for Amateur Photographers.** London, 1890

*Hicks, Wilson. **Words and Pictures.** New York, 1952

Hill, Levi L. and W. McCartey, Jr. **A Treatise on Daguerreotype.** Parts I, II, III, & IV. Lexington, N.Y., 1850

Humphrey, S. D. **American Hand Book of the Daguerreotype.** 5th edition. New York, 1858

Hunt, Robert. **A Manual of Photography.** 3rd edition. London, 1853

Hunt, Robert. **Researches on Light.** London, 1844

Jones, Bernard E., editor. **Cassell's Cyclopaedia of Photography.** London, 1911

Lerebours, N. P. **A Treatise on Photography.** London, 1843

Litchfield, R. B. **Tom Wedgwood, The First Photographer.** London, 1903

Maclean, Hector. **Photography for Artists.** London, 1896

Martin, Paul. **Victorian Snapshots.** London, 1939

Mortensen, William. **Monsters and Madonnas.** San Francisco, 1936

*Nonsilver Printing Processes: Four Selections, 1886-1927. New York, 1973

Ourdan, J. P. **The Art of Retouching by Burrows & Colton.** Revised by the author. 1st American edition. New York, 1880

Potonniée, Georges. **The History of the Discovery of Photography.** New York, 1936

Price, [William] Lake. **A Manual of Photographic Manipulation.** 2nd edition. London, 1868

Pritchard, H. Baden. **About Photography and Photographers.** New York, 1883

Pritchard, H. Baden. **The Photographic Studios of Europe.** London, 1882

Robinson, H[enry] P[each] and Capt. [W. de W.] Abney. **The Art and Practice of Silver Printing.** The American edition. New York, 1881

Robinson, H[enry] P[each]. **The Elements of a Pictorial Photograph.** Bradford, 1898

Robinson, H[enry] P[each]. **Letters on Landscape Photography.** New York, 1888

Robinson, H[enry] P[each]. **Picture-Making by Photography.** 5th edition. London, 1897

Robinson, H[enry] P[each]. **The Studio, and What to Do in It.** London, 1891

Rodgers, H. J. **Twenty-three Years under a Sky-light,** or Life and Experiences of a Photographer. Hartford, Conn., 1872

Roh, Franz and Jan Tschichold, editors. **Foto-auge, Oeil et Photo, Photo-eye.** 76 Photos of the Period. Stuttgart, Ger., 1929

Ryder, James F. **Voigtländer and I:** In Pursuit of Shadow Catching. Cleveland, 1902

Society for Promoting Christian Knowledge. **The Wonders of Light and Shadow.** London, 1851

Sparling, W. **Theory and Practice of the Photographic Art.** London, 1856

Tissandier, Gaston. **A History and Handbook of Photography.** Edited by J. Thomson. 2nd edition. London, 1878

University of Pennsylvania. **Animal Locomotion. The Muybridge Work at the University of Pennsylvania.** Philadelphia, 1888

Vitray, Laura, John Mills, Jr., and Roscoe Ellard. **Pictorial Journalism.** New York and London, 1939

Vogel, Hermann. **The Chemistry of Light and Photography.** New York, 1875

Wall, A. H. **Artistic Landscape Photography.** London, [1896]

Wall, Alfred H. **A Manual of Artistic Colouring, As Applied to Photographs.** London, 1861

Werge, John. **The Evolution of Photography.** London, 1890

Wilson, Edward L. **The American Carbon Manual.** New York, 1868

Wilson, Edward L. **Wilson's Photographics.** New York, 1881

All of the books in the collection are clothbound. An asterisk indicates that the book is also available paperbound.